Krishna's Butter

For the Champion Students

Dr. Bhawana Badhe

Third Edition: January 2025

Second Edition February 2018

Published by

Midam Foundation.

Midam Ashram, RS No. 144/5, Earraikkarai Road,
Kothapurinatham Village,Puducherry 605102

Printed by

Midam Foundation.

Midam Ashram, RS No. 144/5, Earraikkarai Road,
Kothapurinatham Village,Puducherry 605102

First Edition: April 2017

Published and Printed By:

Omji Publishing House Private Limited

Foreword

India's Just like how a grandmother tells her grandchildren a story fully painted with the different colours of creativity, similarly Mrs. Bhawana Badhe has taken a deep subject like the Bhagwad Gita & tried to explain it to children. The Bhagavad Gita consists of 700 shlokas , which normally only people above 40 years take up for study. The mere thought that this can be useful for the character building of children is in itself very beautiful & appreciable. The author has selected around 100 shlokas from the 700 shlokas and explained in simple words as to how they can be useful for children .
The most important message of the Gita is – "Learn , Teach and live as per the teachings of the Gita."

Meaning be like the ideal Arjuna and practically apply these principles and teach others the same and this beautiful message shows how the Guru-Disciple relation can be strengthened. It has been noted by the author with great simplicity.

Arjun, a fighter, a student, who was full of emotions and was in a completely disturbed state of mind received the right guidance from his Guru and made up his mind. The author has very nicely written how even in difficult situations we can direct our inner strength and take the right decision and this she has done through proper explanations of the shlokas.

In this book Karmayoga is explained as "Detachment yet excellence in work with full surrender".

While children focus on increasing their physical abilities and capacities they must also keep in mind that above the senses is the mind and above the mind is the discriminative intelligence and above all these is the Eternal Atma & we should proceed in this direction.

The author has emphasised that after focussing on individual progress , it is the need of the hour to be a global student with a global perspective and this she has done well through the shloka "with regularity in sleep, food ,awakening & work a state of Yoga can be attained "

In the process of learning a strong devotion for the divine is instilled in the children and they also begin to gain knowledge about the Divine qualities, this setup is in itself very excellent. While doing self study the children identify their own nature as per Satva, Rajas,

Tamas and how they can progress with respect to their nature is very well explained. Just as counsellors and psychologists guide children during counselling the same guidance is being given through the shlokas of the Gita.

The author has explained really well how In this whole process of learning every student learns to be like Arjuna and he /she first analyse the situations that comein front of him/her and only then finalise how to handle the situation and proceed ahead.

This book written by Dr.Bhawana under the guidance of her Guru Shri. Madhusudan Damle is worth appreciating and words are not enough to praise this commendable feat.

I would like to once again congratulate the author with all my heart and quote that this book is a master key and I invite the children to receive this book and treat it like a Gita Prasad for their lives.

Shri Ram Moreshwar Khandwe,
Karyavaha Yogabhyasi Madal, Ramnagar, Nagpur
06/08/2017

Author's Note:

I had a strong aspiration that the wisdom of the Gita should reach the children but I did not know how to materialize this thought because I felt its concepts were very advanced for young children. So I approached my teacher Sri.M.R.Damle and sought his help in simplifying the great concepts embedded in the mystic scripture so that it can be easily grasped by children. With his guidance, I began teaching the 9th Class students of 'Vidya Niketan School' in Pondicherry during my lunchbreaks. After completing two batches, some youngsters demanded that I write a book on the same and the notes that were compiled from my lectures became the contents of this book. On the relevance of the Gita in today's world, I quote my teacher's words,

"The Gita is integral in all its principles which can be imbibed by all sections of the society. It teaches a sage to become better sage,a warrior to become better warrior, a businessman to become a better businessman, a politician to become a better politician, a teacher to become a better teacher and a student to become a better student".

Children, The Bhagavad Gita is a timeless book that is both an art as well as a science of living. When we understand about the right attitude towards life, our life gets transformed. The Gita helps us to bring this transformation in life. The Gita introduces us to a role model, Sri Krishna who is the perfect teacher. Arjuna is the example of a sincere student who asks some important questions of life to Krishna and Krishna teaches Arjuna that the best way to live is by becoming a perfect student. If we cultivate this attitude and aspire to become a perfect student throughout our life, our life can certainly be transformed.

This book is dedicated to all the sincere students who wish to understand the words of Sri Krishna, who narrated The Bhagavad Gita to his disciple - Arjuna, in the middle of the battlefield during the mighty battle of Kurukshetra. The aim of this book is to inspire the children of today to become super students.

Tomorrow's nation is in today's classrooms and today's children have a very essential role to play tomorrow. Verses of the Bhagavad Gita have been selected which are applicable for the students to help them understand the practical philosophy in dealing with parents, teacher, society and the world at large.

An attempt has been made to put these shlokas in the rhyme form so that they can be easily understood and I have selected some special verses which are most applicable for today's children.

I begin with a sincere appeal to the students for reading the message from this Gita Study which I shall call "GITA PRASAD" as this truly holds a potential to bring a great transformation in your lives.

***

Introduction: The Battle Begins!

"Mahabharata, the greatest epic of India which is actually a very long poem in Sanskrit language comprising of One lakh verses, was compiled by the legendary sage Vyasa. The epic Mahabharata has 18 Parvas or Parts. In the Bhishmaparva or the Part on Bhishma, the 700 verses of the Bhagavad Gita can be found. The Bhagavad Gita in turn is divided into 18 Adhyayas or Chapters.

The Kauravas and Pandavas, the two sections of the Kuru Clan had assembled to fight at the war field of Kurukshetra near Hastinapur (modern day Delhi). The blind Emperor Dhritarashtra had decided to hand over his throne to Yudhishthira the eldest Pandava and not his own son Duryodhana who had evil qualities. But Duryodhana cunningly secured the throne for himself and resorted to all sorts of trickery and deceit to eliminate the Pandavas who had divine traits of purity and virtue.

The Divine Krishna who was an impartial friend of the Kuru Clan approached Duryodhana and suggested to him to give five small villages to the five Pandava Princes. However, Duryodhana refused to give even a needle tip of land to the Pandavas and this then led to the great battle at Kurukshetra. All the kings and master warriors and teachers then got involved in this battle and chose one of the two sides. The common military teacher of the Pandavas and Kauravas, Dronacharya and also the senior-most grandsire Bhishma chose the side of the Kauravas to fulfil their personal pledges and promises. Krishna declared that he would himself not participate in the battle. However he offered a choice to both the sides. The choice was either Sri Krishna himself or his large army. Duryodhana chose the mighty army of Krishna and Arjuna chose to have Krishna by his side and so, Krishna became the charioteer of Arjuna during the battle.

And it is in the middle of the battle field that the Bhagavad Gita began with this verse where Dhritarashtra asked the oracle Sanjay who had been blessed with a supernormal vision and foresight.

***

धृतराष्ट्र उवाच
धर्मक्षेत्रे कुरुक्षेत्रे समवेता युयुत्सवः ।
मामकाः पाण्डवाश्चैव किमकुर्वत सञ्जय ॥ १-१॥

dhṛtarāṣṭra uvāca
dharmakṣetre kurukṣetre samavetā yuyutsavaḥ
māmakāḥ pāṇḍavāś caiva kim akurvata sañjaya 1.1

"Gathered together in Kurukshetra to battle
Assembled eagerly to prove their mettle
The Pandavas and my Kauravas poised for a fight
O Sanjay! What happened there? Share your Divine sight |1|"

Children, with this introduction let us now begin to understand the Gita and its practical principles which are very applicable in our everyday lives. Just like the Pandavas and Kauravas engaged in Battle in Kurukshetra, all of us have to wage a battle on the inside at one point or the other. This battle is the battle between good and bad. This book will help you in this inner battle so that you can ensure that the champions and heroes who are inside you will always guide you in the right direction in life.

***

Lesson 1 - I Adhyaya of the Gita

"If we cannot find any solution, we must never hesitate to ask for help to a teacher or an elder or even a trusted friend"

Lesson 1: Adhyaya : 1
The Grief of Arjuna

Just before the battle began, Arjuna asked Krishna to take his chariot into the centre of the battlefield. He wanted to see all the warriors on the enemy lines so that he could be prepared for the battle. But when Krishna brought the chariot to the centre, Arjuna saw his own friends and elders and relatives standing on the other side of the battle field. Even though he was fully aware of who his opponents were beforehand, Arjuna became nervous in the last minute on seeing all of them. In his nervousness, he became anxious and his Gandiva-Bow slipped from his hand and fell down and Arjuna's throat became very dry. He already imagined that he had lost the battle and sorrowfully sat down and bluntly told Krishna that he would not participate in the battle. Sometimes we see that just before an important occasion like an examination or a sports event or a cultural function, the persons who have an important role begin to feel very nervous. Arjuna too developed a similar feeling, but the only difference was that his nervousness was very dangerous as it was likely to lead to the loss of many lives of his armed warriors. Many times in life we find that despite our best efforts we face very huge challenges and at these times, even though we feel sad and depressed, it is very important that we should not give up. If we cannot find any solution, we must never hesitate to ask help to a teacher or an elder or even a trusted friend. Arjuna too did not understand what he was supposed to do as he could not prepare himself to participate in the battle. So he shared his grief with Krishna who was his teacher, elder and also his dearest friend.

***

Canto One: **The Grief of Arjuna**

अथ प्रथमोऽध्यायः।

atha prathamodhyāyaḥ

हृषीकेशं तदा वाक्यमिदमाह महीपते।
अर्जुन उवाच।
सेनयोरुभयोर्मध्ये रथं स्थापय मेऽच्युत ॥१-२१॥

hṛṣīkeśaṃ tadā vākyam idam āha mahīpate
arjuna uvāca senayor ubhayor madhye rathaṃ sthāpaya mecyuta 1.21

O King! Then to the Divine charioteer *Krishna*,
The following words were spoken by *Arjuna*
"Between the two armies, I request you to take
Our chariot, into the battle-field's center for my sake|21|

यावदेतान्निरीक्षेऽहं योद्धुकामानवस्थितान्।
कैर्मया सह योद्धव्यमस्मिन् रणसमुद्यमे ॥१-२२॥

yāvad etān nirikṣehaṃ yoddhukāmān avasthitān
kair mayā saha yoddhavyam asmin raṇasamudyame 1.22

Unless this warfield, I closely observe and see
Those who desire to wage the battle against me,
I cannot assess the warriors' strength and might
And decide the opponents who are worthy to fight|22|

गाण्डीवं स्रंसते हस्तात्त्वक्चैव परिदह्यते।
न च शक्नोम्यवस्थातुं भ्रमतीव च मे मनः ॥१-३०॥

gāṇḍīvaṃ straṃsate hastāt tvak caiva paridahyate
na ca śaknomy avasthātuṃ bhramatīva ca me manaḥ 1.30

From my hands, slips the *Gandiva* bow
And my skin-seems on fire now!
My mind and head are spinning round
Impossible it is for me to even stand ground!|30|

सञ्जय उवाच।

एवमुक्त्वार्जुनः सङ्ख्ये रथोपस्थ उपाविशत्।

विसृज्य सशरं चापं शोकसंविग्नमानसः ॥१-४७॥

sañjaya uvāca

evam uktvārjunaḥ saṇkhye rathopastha upāviśat

visṛjya saśaraṃ cāpaṃ śokasaṃvignamānasaḥ 1.47

Sanjaya spoke:

"After saying so, *Arjuna*, amidst the war-field

His bow and arrows he refused to wield

Dropping down on to his chariot's seat

In delusion he had already considered defeat.|47|"

***

Lesson 2.1 - Upholding one's Duties

Art by Somkanta Chaterjee

"One must always remember that the most important duty of every individual is to stand by the side of truth and uphold what is right!"

Lesson : 2 (Part I) Adhyaya : 2
Krishna Reveals Eternal Secrets

The Second adhyaya of The Bhagavad Gita begins by narrating the condition of the best warrior Arjuna going into depression after seeing that he has to fight all his elders and brothers and in-laws and nephews present in the opposite camp in the war .

Here one must know the reason for Arjuna's sorrow. Because of his emotions towards his kinsmen, Arjuna's mind became clouded. Becoming emotional is not the main problem because feeling emotions is a natural human experience, but when one neglects one's duties completely because of emotions, then it becomes a great problem. Even though Arjuna was fully deluded and unable to understand what his right course of action was, he was wise enough to reach out for help and so he sought the help of his dearest friend and teacher, the Divine Krishna and so Krishna came to his rescue.

The helpless and confused Arjuna sought refuge of his charioteer Krishna and in an action of surrender told him, “Show the way, teacher”. A lot of people think surrendering to a knowledgeable teacher or a wise elder is equal to surrendering to a strong enemy. But in reality it is quite different. There is a lot of happiness in taking refuge in the shelter of wise and experienced persons. One can relate better if one understands this simple classroom example. If a student has to learn a theorem in mathematics, he must surrender to the teacher without arrogance or resistance. And he must try to sincerely understand the methodology used in solving the theorem. But if the student simply criticizes his teacher's methodology and tries to find faults in the teacher's ways, he will only end up learning nothing and will never be benefited from the teacher's experience and wisdom. Likewise all great leaders have been great students first and it is always best to have a student's attitude throughout life.

In the Gita, Krishna counseled Arjuna and said, “The wise grieve not and know that the soul never expires.” He told Arjuna that the body passes through phases like childhood, youth and old age but the soul or the "Atman" that silently resides inside everyone never dies.

The soul takes on another body just like a person changes his shirt when it is worn out. He advised Arjuna to not grieve because it is the fact that for one who takes birth, death is certain and for the one who dies, birth is certain .This is an important message from Gita as it takes away all the fear of death and one can understand that death is not "The End" but the continuation of a journey. This ancient secret revealed by Krishna is called the Sankhya Yoga in the Gita.

Krishna then told Arjuna that no matter what situation arises, one must not fail to perform one's duty at all times. One must always remember that the most important duty of every individual is to stand by the side of truth and uphold what is right!

***

Canto II: **Eternal Secrets Revealed** (Part I)

कार्पण्यदोषोपहतस्वभावः पृच्छामि त्वां धर्मसम्मूढचेताः ।
यच्छ्रेयः स्यान्निश्चितं ब्रूहि तन्मे शिष्यस्तेऽहं शाधि मां त्वां प्रपन्नम् ॥२-७॥

kārpaṇyadoṣopahatasvabhāvaḥ pṛcchāmi tvāṃ
dharmasaṃmūḍhacetāḥ yac chreyaḥ syān niścitaṃ brūhi tan me
śiṣyasteham śādhi māṃ tvāṃ prapannam 2.7

I ask to you in this state of confusion-
Tell me my right course of action
Thus afflicted and infected by fear,
I seek your refuge; Show the way- teacher! |7|

श्रीभगवानुवाच।
देहिनोऽस्मिन्यथा देहे कौमारं यौवनं जरा।
तथा देहान्तरप्राप्तिर्धीरस्तत्र न मुह्यति ॥२-१३॥

dehinosmin yathā dehe kaumāraṃ yauvanaṃ jarā
tathā dehāntaraprāptir dhīras tatra na muhyati 2.13

Krishna said:
Just as our soul, when in this body silently resides
Childhood, youth and old-age it consensually abides
After leaving this body, another one it requires
The wise grieve not and know that the soul never expires.|13|

नासतो विद्यते भावो नाभावो विद्यते सतः ।
उभयोरपि दृष्टोऽन्तस्त्वनयोस्तत्त्वदर्शिभिः ॥ २-१६॥

nāsato vidyate bhāvo nābhāvo vidyate sataḥ
ubhayor api dṛṣṭo.antas tv anayos tattvadarśibhiḥ 2.16

Falsehood is that which holds no authority
And truth is omnipresent in every territory.
The essence of both have been shown
By the wisest of seers to whom it was known|16|

वासांसि जीर्णानि यथा विहाय नवानि गृह्णाति नरोऽपराणि ।
तथा शरीराणि विहाय जीर्णान्यन्यानि संयाति नवानि देही ॥ २-२२॥

vāsāṃsi jīrṇāni yathā vihāya navāni gṛhṇāti naroparāṇi
that ā śarīrāṇi vihāya jīrṇāni anyāni saṃyāti navāni dehī 2.22

Just like old garments are discarded when shoddy
And thus for newer clothes they make way
The old physical bodies too are cast away
By the 'Self' which then acquires a new body.|22|

स्वधर्ममपि चावेक्ष्य न विकम्पितुमर्हसि ।
धर्म्याद्धि युद्धाच्छ्रेयोऽन्यत्क्षत्रियस्य न विद्यते ॥ २-३१॥

svadharmam api cāvekṣya na vikampitum arhasi
dharmyād dhi yuddhāc chreyonyat kṣatriyasya na vidyate 2.31

Your Dharma- moral duty you must consider
And from it you most definitely mustn't falter
For the warriors who – to uphold the truth fight
Nothing is most appropriate but to defend the right! |31|

***

Lesson 2.2- The Foundation of Karma Yoga- The Yoga of Action

"Detachment yet excellence in work is the real Yoga of Action."

Lesson : 2 (Part II) Adhyaya : 2
The Foundation of Karma Yoga

In this part of the second Adhyaya, Krishna told Arjuna that the secret of Karma yoga or The Yoga of Action lies in performing one's duties in a proper manner. He said that when the most basic things are done perfectly, our actions can produce extra-ordinary outcomes.

Sometimes, we see that children do their homework or any work in return for a promised reward or a gift eg.a chocolate. Unknowingly the children become dependant on the rewards for performing their task and then they lose interest in their work and become spoilt. Having a liking for something is okay but when the liking grows into desire, it gets converted into greed. Greed and Desire are responsible for most of the problems in today's world.

So, while performing any action, it is important that we must not do any action just for the sake of the reward we expect in return for our work.This is because the desire for fruits distracts us from work.If we are not motivated by the fruits of our actions, we can perform our duties in a more efficient way. Before every action if one is attached to fruits, one's mind gets carried away and then the action itself becomes defective. When one gets detached from the desire of the fruits of action, one is peaceful and happy and can perform excellent work. In the true sense, detachment means working with full enthusiasm irrespective of the results. The aim and focus of detached action is perfection and not just some outer reward. Detachment yet excellence in work is the real Yoga of Action. This is the foundation of the Karma Yoga of the Bhagavad Gita.

If you observe a captain of a sporting team or a commander in the army or a leader of any organization - you will find that they all have one thing in common. All follow and practice this principle of detachment. This is because having a calm mind is important in pressure situations. When you are peaceful you can find the solution to any problem.

If you get angry and disturbed during difficult situations, you can neither solve the problem nor be a good leader and guide others in finding a solution.

When you see that a person remains calm at all times and does not get excited by success or depressed by failure, you can understand that such a person is worthy of being called a true champion. As per the Gita, such a person is fit to be called a Muni - a true sage!

***

Canto II: **Eternal Secrets Revealed** (Part II)

नेहाभिक्रमनाशोऽस्ति प्रत्यवायो न विद्यते।
स्वल्पमप्यस्य धर्मस्य त्रायते महतो भयात्॥ २-४०॥

nehābhikramanāśosti pratyavāyo na vidyate
svalpam apy asya dharmasya trāyate mahato bhayāt 2.40

Here, the actions once begun bring no losses
Or any negative results or consequences
Even the smallest action done in the right manner
Can protect one from the greatest danger|40|

कर्मण्येवाधिकारस्ते मा फलेषु कदाचन।
मा कर्मफलहेतुर्भूर्मा ते सङ्गोऽस्त्वकर्मणि ॥ २-४७॥

karmaṇy evādhikāras te mā phaleṣu kadācana
mā karmaphalahetur bhūr mā te saṇgostv akarmaṇi 2.47

Vested you are with the authority to perform
But not seek your action's fruits in any form
When by the fruits of actions you aren't motivated
From discharging your duties, you never get deviated |47|

बुद्धियुक्तो जहातीह उभे सुकृतदुष्कृते।
तस्माद्योगाय युज्यस्व योगः कर्मसु कौशलम्॥२-५०॥

buddhi-yukto jahātīha ubhe sukṛta-duṣkṛte tasmād yogāya yujyasva
yogaḥ karmasu kauśalam 2.50

With this knowledge, in this very world itself
From good and bad actions, one can free oneself.
Knowing this, engage yourself in this Karma-Yoga
Detachment yet excellence in works is only Yoga |50|

दुःखेष्वनुद्विग्नमनाः सुखेषु विगतस्पृहः ।
वीतरागभयक्रोधः स्थितधीर्मुनिरुच्यते ॥ २-५६॥

duḥkheṣvanudvignamanāḥ sukheṣu vigataspṛhaḥ
vītarāgabhayakrodhaḥ sthitadhīr munir ucyate 2.56

When one suffers not in times of distress
And in happiness, exuberance one doesn't express
When you see someone free from anger and fear
It is clearly understood that a sage is near.|56|

***

Lesson 3- Listening to the Divine being inside us

"If we listen to the Divine being inside us, our journey towards happiness is fastest because the Driver is the Divine Himself."

Lesson : 3 Adhyaya : 3
Listening to the Divine Being Inside Us

Arjuna was very confused. On one side Krishna had asked him to become detached and peaceful and on another side, he had instructed him to perform his duty of participating in the war. He thought both are not possible at once. So he asked Krishna, "You say that spiritual knowledge is superior to material action then why are you asking me to participate in the battle?"

A smiling Krishna told Arjuna that no moment can pass on earth without an action being performed. At any instant, There is always something happening even when a man does not perform outward action, an internal action takes place eg. thoughts, digestion etc. This is a quality of Nature which cannot be changed. Krishna told Arjuna that one can never give up actions totally and action was always superior to in action. Action gives experience and strength even in day to day life and without action no accomplishment is possible.

If we become detached, we can perform action with a spirit of freedom and every action becomes a spiritual action. This way we can not only perform action but also be free at the same time. There is a Divine being who is beyond the understanding of our mind and also beyond our five senses. This divine being is inside all of us. Different people call him by different names. To make Arjuna understand, Krishna offered a simple formula. He told that we must contemplate upon the Divine being present inside us and we must offer all works to Him and perform our actions. If we listen to the Divine being inside us, our journey towards happiness is fastest because the Driver is the Divine Himself.

***

Canto III: **Unveiling the Spirit in Material Action**

अथ तृतीयोऽध्यायः ।
atha tṛtīyodhyāyaḥ

अर्जुन उवाच।
ज्यायसी चेत्कर्मणस्ते मता बुद्धिर्जनार्दन।
तत्किं कर्मणि घोरे मां नियोजयसि केशव ॥३-१॥

arjuna uvāca
jyāyasī cet karmaṇas te matā buddhir janārdana
tat kiṃ karmaṇi ghore māṃ niyojayasi keśava 3.1

Arjuna asked:
"O *Krishna*, Haven't you just said what is superior,
That spiritual knowledge over material action is better!
Then why is it that you coerce me into action?
This ghastly *"karma"* on me, why do you sanction? |1|

न हि कश्चित्क्षणमपि जातु तिष्ठत्यकर्मकृत्।
कार्यते ह्यवशः कर्म सर्वः प्रकृतिजैर्गुणैः ॥३-५॥

na hi kaścit kṣaṇamapi jātu tiṣṭhatyakarmakṛt
kāryate hy avaśaḥ karma sarvaḥ prakṛtijair guṇaiḥ 3.5

Not a single such moment can pass for man
As without engaging in activity, exist- no one can
This nature's qualities on all beings has been endowed-
A bond of works and actions on man has been bestowed.|5|

नियतं कुरु कर्म त्वं कर्म ज्यायो ह्यकर्मणः।
शरीरयात्रापि च ते न प्रसिद्ध्येदकर्मणः ॥३-८॥

niyataṃ kuru karma tvaṃ karma jyāyo hy akarmaṇaḥ
śarīrayātrāpi ca te na prasidhyedakarmaṇaḥ 3.8

Without attachment, perform your every action
Because action always supersedes inaction
Even your body's life journey cannot be sustained
Without action no accomplishment can be attained.|8|

मयि सर्वाणि कर्माणि संन्यस्याध्यात्मचेतसा।
निराशीर्निर्ममो भूत्वा युध्यस्व विगतज्वरः ॥३-३०॥

mayi sarvāṇi karmāṇi saṃnyasyādhyātmacetasā
nirāśīr nirmamo bhūtvā yudhyasva vigatajvaraḥ 3.30

Consecrating your actions to Me (the supreme I),
Meditate upon your 'Self' that is a part of Me
Without holding on to desires or prestige
Without grief or remorse, ready your weapons to lay siege|30|

इन्द्रियाणि पराण्याहुरिन्द्रियेभ्यः परं मनः।
मनसस्तु परा बुद्धिर्यो बुद्धेः परतस्तु सः ॥३-४२॥

indriyāṇi parāṇy āhur indriyebhyaḥ paraṃ manaḥ
manasas tu parā buddhir yo buddheḥ paratas tu saḥ 3.42

Beyond the senses that are supreme is the mind
Beyond the mind –the awakened intelligence you find
But beyond the awakened intelligence it is thus said-
It is He- the eternal "Self"- the supreme Godhead.|42|

***

Lesson 4- There is a champion inside all of us

"When man can awaken the godly trait inside,
every human being has the potential to be a divine representative on earth."

Lesson : 4 Adhyaya : 4
There is a Champion Inside All of Us

Krishna promised Arjuna that whenever there was an increase in darkness and pain among the people of the earth, an Avataar or a Divine representative would come to the front to bring a great transformation. This truth which was said many thousand years ago is very valid today also. But the burning question is how we can conceive the idea of avatar in today's time. There is a lot of darkness in the form of ignorance in the minds of the people of our world and a lot of good people are suffering because of this. As there are so many problems it seems to solve all the problems that our world is facing, we need more than one divine representative.

We have seen that, whenever there is natural calamity or disaster, people come together and we see the godly qualities surface in times of crisis. During the Chennai floods in 2016, we saw how ordinary people joined and selflessly worked for many days leaving aside their homes without looking at caste, creed, religion or region and saved thousands of people. Selflessly working for the betterment of others is a godly trait and this must be respected.

When man can awaken the godly trait inside, every human being has the potential to be a divine representative on earth. Last chapter, we studied that there is a divine being inside us whom we can awaken by performing actions in a detached manner. In this chapter Krishna further explains that we can do this by inculcating good qualities in us. If we can offer all our works to the Divine and perform every action without fear, anger, desire or expectation and be calm in both success and failure and be always cheerful, we can all lead a Divine life.

***

Canto IV : **Krishna Opens The Doors of Knowledge**

अथ चतुर्थोऽध्यायः।

atha caturthodhyāyaḥ

यदा यदा हि धर्मस्य ग्लानिर्भवति भारत।

अभ्युत्थानमधर्मस्य तदात्मानं सृजाम्यहम् ॥४-७॥

yadā yadā hi dharmasya glānir bhavati bhārata
abhyutthānam adharmasya tadātmānaṃ sṛjāmy aham 4.7

At all times when righteousness is at its wane
O Child of Light, whenever there is a reign of darkness and pain
When injustice and entropy blares on the human side-
My *Avataar* descends into the mortal realm to turn the tide.|7|

वीतरागभयक्रोधा मन्मया मामुपाश्रिताः।

बहवो ज्ञानतपसा पूता मद्भावमागताः ॥४-१०॥

vītarāgabhayakrodhā manmayā mām upāśritāḥ
bahavo jñānatapasā pūtā madbhāvam āgatāḥ 4.10

Thus exempted from attachment, fear and anger
With their minds seeking refuge in My shelter
Such men of knowledge who have performed penance-
In divinizing life, they have been able to advance.|10|

यस्य सर्वे समारम्भाः कामसङ्कल्पवर्जिताः।

ज्ञानाग्निदग्धकर्माणं तमाहुः पण्डितं बुधाः ॥४-१९॥

yasya sarve samārambhāḥ kāmasaṃkalpavarjitāḥ
jñānāgnidagdhakarmāṇaṃ tam āhuḥ paṇḍitaṃ budhāḥ 4.19

He who seeks not any gratification
He whose every activity is without desire
He whose very works are consumed by knowledge's fire
He is declared to be the wisest sage in action.|19|

यदृच्छालाभसन्तुष्टो द्वन्द्वातीतो विमत्सरः ।
समः सिद्धावसिद्धौ च कृत्वापि न निबध्यते ॥४-२२॥

yadṛcchālābhasaṃtuṣṭo dvandvātīto vimatsaraḥ
samaḥ siddhāv asiddhau ca kṛtvāpi na nibadhyate 4.22

With whatever good that naturally comes his way
He is contented, thus never envious on any day
Both success and failure, he greets with poise
Works don't bind him for he has transcended choice.|22|

***

Lesson 5 - Controlling Desire and Anger

*"If we want to be free and joyous in life,
we must control both desire and anger."*

Lesson : 5 Adhyaya : 5
Controlling Desire and Anger

Arjuna asked Krishna to once more explain what was better for him- renunciation or divine action. Krishna explained to him that even though both renunciation and divine action ultimately help a human being in becoming fully free, the path of divine action is the best way. It is only by performing right actions that a person can attain true realization. When a person gets this realization, everything begins to appear as equal and one. From the learned man to the mighty elephant, from the cow to the dog and creatures eating lower animals, all begin to appear as same. This is because the liberated person can understand that in all living creatures there is the same divinity.

Krishna reveals a very straightforward way in which anybody can be free and enjoy life truly. He says that both desire and anger flow in a sudden rush. If a person can control his desire and anger and be steady at all times, he can attain the highest realization that is possible to man and he can experience a wonderful happiness throughout his life.

While studying for examinations, many times we get a very strong desire to play or go outdoors instead of studying. Sometimes when our things don't happen as per our wish or if our dear ones do not listen to us, we get very angry. In both situations, if we allow our desire or anger to lead us we will either end up performing badly in examinations or spoil our relationships with our friends and elders.

If we want to be free and joyous in life, we must control both desire and anger. The best way to do so is by doing our every action as an offering. When our mother or father cooks food for us, they make the best for us. In a similar way, if we can imagine that we are offering everything we do to a best friend who is sitting inside us, we can always peform our best and in this way we will be joyous and peaceful.

***

Canto V: **Absolute Renunciation**

अथ पञ्चमोऽध्यायः।

atha pañcamodhyāyaḥ

श्रीभगवानुवाच।
संन्यासः कर्मयोगश्च निःश्रेयसकरावुभौ।
तयोस्तु कर्मसंन्यासात्कर्मयोगो विशिष्यते ॥५-२॥

śrībhagavān uvāca
saṃnyāsaḥ karmayogaś ca niḥśreyasakarāv ubhau
tayos tu karmasaṃnyāsāt karmayogo viśiṣyate 5.2

Lord *Krishna* replied:
"The path of Divine action and the way of renunciation-
Both these two lead to the ultimate liberation
But amongst all paths if one were to choose the best
The way of Divine union in activities is superior to the rest.|2|

विद्याविनयसम्पन्ने ब्राह्मणे गवि हस्तिनि।
शुनि चैव श्वपाके च पण्डिताः समदर्शिनः ॥५-१८॥

vidyāvinayasampanne brāhmaṇe gavi hastini
śuni caiva śvapāke ca paṇḍitāḥ samadarśinaḥ 5.18

Those whose eyes are illumined with that knowledge's insight
All living ones appear equivalent and identical to their sight-
From the learned spiritual seeker to the elephant or the cow
From the dog to the consumers of lower animals like the sow.|18|

शक्नोतीहैव यः सोढुं प्राकशरीरविमोक्षणात्।
कामक्रोधोद्भवं वेगं स युक्तः स सुखी नरः ॥५-२३॥

śaknotīhaiva yaḥ soḍhuṃ prāk śarīravimokṣaṇāt
kāmakrodhodbhavaṃ vegaṃ sa yuktaḥ sa sukhī naraḥ 5.23

He who is able to bear and sustain,
The rush of anger and the gush of desire
In this very birth itself he shall obtain-
The highest realization of bliss that man can acquire.|23|

Lesson 6- Developing a Global Perspective

Art by Priti Pandurangan

"A global-student does not discriminate on the basis of religion, stature, caste, society or even nation as he knows that all are just the same from the inside."

Lesson : 6 Adhyaya : 6
Developing a Global Perspective

This Adhyaya teaches us about the importance of maintaining discipline in our lives. We can achieve great wonders if we perform all our activities as offerings to the Divine without expecting any rewards in return for a work. With regularity in action and by making sacrifice, a person can widen his mind and improve his understanding.

With punctuality and regularity if we eat, sleep and work, our mind also becomes regulated and sorrow disappears from life. If a student practices this discipline in his life, his mind also expands and he becomes more tolerant. He begins to understand that the same Divine being that is present inside him is also present inside every living thing.

Such a student does not discriminate on the basis of religion, stature, caste or society or even nation as he knows that all are just the way he is from the inside.

When a student follows a disciplined life and without expectation accepts everyone with tolerance, he does not discriminate between himself and others and he becomes a global-student. The need of the hour is that students should develop a global and universal perspective.

***

Canto VI:**The Merger with the Supernal Divine:**

अथ षष्ठोऽध्यायः।

atha ṣaṣṭhodhyāyaḥ

श्रीभगवानुवाच।
अनाश्रितः कर्मफलं कार्यं कर्म करोति यः ।
स संन्यासी च योगी च न निरग्निर्न चाक्रियः ॥६-१॥

śrībhagavān uvāca
anāśritaḥ karmaphalaṃ kāryaṃ karma karoti yaḥ
sa saṃnyāsī ca yogī ca na niragnir na cākriyaḥ 6.1

Sri Krishna said:
"He who dutifully works without desire
Him- the expectations of fruits cannot cage

And he is said to be the *Sannyasin*- the *Yogi* –the real sage.
Not he who renounces actions and kindles not the sacrificial fire .|1|

युक्ताहारविहारस्य युक्तचेष्टस्य कर्मसु।
युक्तस्वप्नावबोधस्य योगो भवति दुःखहा ॥६-१७॥

yuktāhāravihārasya yuktaceṣṭasya karmasu
yuktasvapnāvabodhasya yogo bhavati duḥkhahā 6.17

All sorrows begin to cease and disappear
When the state of *Yoga* approaches near
Wherein the sleep, awakening and food is in regulation
And works too, when the mind engages in regulated action.|17|

सर्वभूतस्थमात्मानं सर्वभूतानि चात्मनि।
ईक्षते योगयुक्तात्मा सर्वत्र समदर्शनः ॥६-२९॥

sarvabhūtastham ātmānaṃ sarvabhūtāni cātmani
īkṣate yogayuktātmā sarvatra samadarśanaḥ 6.29

Such a man who has attained the union universal
Acquires he, a perspective equal and global-
For he sees the Self in all and all in the Self
And he discriminates not others from himself |29|

***

Lesson 7 - The Universal Divine Existence

Art by Somkanta Chaterjee

*"Whatever is finest and pure in the world,
we can simply understand and recognize it to be
essentially Divine."*

Lesson : 7 Adhyaya : 7
The Universal Divine Existence

The word Yoga literally means 'union' and Krishna in this chapter declared the science of the union with the Divine. He told Arjuna that Divinity is omnipresent in the universe. It is everywhere- from the taste and the flavor of the waters to the heavenly bodies like the sun and the moon, from the sound of the creation of the universe to the vitality of mankind there is a universal divinity. Whatever is finest and pure in the world, we can simply understand and recognize it to be essentially Divine. One can see this oneness when one smells the best fragrance or even feels the warmth and radiance of fire. When Krishna spoke to Arjuna by saying 'I' am present everywhere and that all the world's existence is sustained by 'Me', the words 'I' and 'Me' refer to the Divine Omnipresent being.

He further told Arjuna that it is the Divine that provides strength to the mighty and that there is only one desire that is permitted and is not wrong. This Desire is the desire to do one's Dharma or moral Duty. Everybody has a dharma to follow. Eg. A student's dharma is to study, a teacher's is to teach, a politician's is to lead his followers in the right manner, a doctor's dharma is to cure patients and a soldier's dharma is to defend his countrymen.

This question can arise in our minds. If everyone has different dharmas how can we all be united? The answer too is provided in the Gita where Krishna said that the highest dharma is to work for the betterment of humanity. If all of us perform our individual dharmas with this aim in mind, we can all be truly united ! Krishna said that the men of virtue who selflessly perform the right deeds are always free from the bonds of any type of sin because they do not have any other material desire or need.

He said that such men are the wise men who have a firm belief in the universal existence of the Divine and so they worship the Divine in the universe with devotion.

***

Canto VII: **The Union Through Knowledge**

अथ सप्तमोऽध्यायः।
atha saptamodhyāyaḥ

ज्ञानं तेऽहं सविज्ञानमिदं वक्ष्याम्यशेषतः।
यज्ज्ञात्वा नेह भूयोऽन्यज्ज्ञातव्यमवशिष्यते ॥७-२॥

jñānaṃ tehaṃ savijñānam idaṃ vakṣyāmy aśeṣataḥ
yaj jñātvā neha bhūyo.anyaj jñātavyam avaśiṣyate 7.2

That science of union to you I shall explain
That which by engaging in *Yoga*, one can attain
That undiluted knowledge after which doubts won't persist
That knowledge beyond which nothing does exist |2|

रसोऽहमप्सु कौन्तेय प्रभास्मि शशिसूर्ययोः।
प्रणवः सर्ववेदेषु शब्दः खे पौरुषं नृषु ॥७-८॥

raso.aham apsu kaunteya prabhāsmi śaśisūryayoḥ
praṇavaḥ sarvavedeṣu śabdaḥ khe pauruṣaṃ nṛṣu 7.8

In the flavor and taste of the waters it is I
O *Arjuna*, I am the light of the sun and moon in the sky
The primordial word of genesis – I am Om- the Vedic sound
The manhood in man and in ether's subsonic element, I am found|8|

पुण्योगन्धः पृथिव्यां च तेजश्चास्मि विभावसौ।
जीवनं सर्वभूतेषु तपश्चास्मि तपस्विषु ॥७-९॥

puṇyo gandhaḥ pṛthivyāṃ ca tejaś cāsmi vibhāvasau
jīvanaṃ sarvabhūteṣu tapaś cāsmi tapasviṣu 7.9

On the earth, I am the purest original fragrance
And for the fire that burns, I am its heat and radiance
I am the vitality that nourishes all beings living
I strengthen the ascetic who is askesis performing |9|

बलं बलवतां चाहं कामरागविवर्जितम्।
धर्माविरुद्धो भूतेषु कामोऽस्मि भरतर्षभ ॥७-११॥

balaṃ balavatāṃ cāhaṃ kāmarāgavivarjitam
dharmāviruddho bhūteṣu kāmo.asmi bharatarṣabha 7.11

I am the strength of the mighty and strong
Devoid of attachment and passion
O *Arjuna*, I am the energy of procreation
I am the *Dharma's* desire that is not wrong |11|

येषां त्वन्तगतं पापं जनानां पुण्यकर्मणाम्।
ते द्वन्द्वमोहनिर्मुक्ता भजन्ते मां दृढव्रताः ॥७-२८॥

yeṣāṃ tv antagataṃ pāpaṃ janānāṃ puṇyakarmaṇām
te dvandvamohanirmuktā bhajante māṃ dṛḍhavratāḥ 7.28

But those virtuous men who are from sin freed,
Who have given up their every material need
Steadfastly they believe in My overlordship
And engage devotedly in My worship|28|

***

Lesson 8 - Performing Divine Action

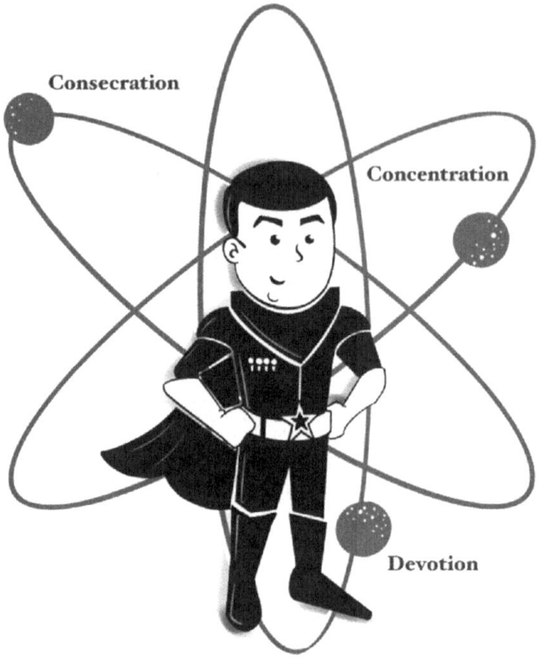

Art by Somkanta Chaterjee

" Concentration, Devotion and Consecration are the three qualities that Krishna identifies to be most beneficial and important for champions."

Lesson : 8 Adhyaya : 8
Performing Divine Action

Three verses from the VIII Adhyaya of the Gita have been selected as they were found to be most relevant from a student's viewpoint. They will be elaborated in this lesson.

Concentration, Devotion and Consecration are the three qualities that Krishna identified to be most beneficial and important for champions. Krishna told Arjuna that if he could have these three qualities while performing his every action he could reach the highest stature. As goes the proverb “As you think, so you become!”. If we constantly think about something, we become closer and similar to the object of our thoughts and admiration.

Without concentration, nothing can be done effectively in the world. When an action is performed with sincerity and love, it becomes a devoted action. When an action is done as an offering irrespective of the end result, the action is done in a state of Consecration.

When an action is done with concentration, devotion and consecration, the action becomes Divine Action. Krishna advised Arjuna that if he constantly remembered the Divine and performed his every action as an offering to Him, he too could become united and one with the Divine. In a similar manner, if students always think of the Divine in all their moments whether while at play or while studying and on all occasions happy or sad, the students can become Divine students. Divine students are the true champions of transformation and they are going to play a major role in making our world a better place.

***

Canto VIII: **Performing Divine Action**

अथ अष्टमोऽध्यायः।

atha aṣṭamodhyāyaḥ

तस्मात्सर्वेषु कालेषु मामनुस्मर युध्य च।
मय्यर्पितमनो बुद्धिर्मा मेवैष्यस्य संशयम् ॥८-७॥

tasmāt sarveṣu kāleṣu mām anusmara yudhya ca
mayy arpitamanobuddhir mām evaiṣyasy asaṃśayaḥ 8.7

In all your battles and actions, let your insight be fixed
Upon Me let your mind and intellect be affixed
At all times when you remember me constantly
O *Arjuna*, you shall then come to Me certainly |7|

अभ्यासयोगयुक्तेन चेतसा नान्यगामिना।
परमं पुरुषं दिव्यं याति पार्थानुचिन्तयन् ॥८-८॥

abhyāsayogayuktena cetasā nānyagāminā
paramaṃ puruṣaṃ divyaṃ yāti pārthānucintayan 8.8

O *Arjuna*, by regulated efforts of consecration
With the mind devoted in concentration
When one practices *Yoga* seeking the union Divine
He merges into the supreme consciousness of Mine|8|

अनन्यचेताः सततं यो मां स्मरति नित्यशः।
तस्याहं सुलभः पार्थ नित्ययुक्तस्य योगिनः ॥८-१४॥

ananyacetāḥ satataṃ yo māṃ smarati nityaśaḥ
tasyāhaṃ sulabhaḥ pārtha nityayuktasya yoginaḥ 8.14

He who practices *Yoga* with an un-deviated mind
Striving to merge his consciousness with Me , him you'll find
In whose memory My remembrance never does cease
He, O *Arjuna*, can attain the union in Me with ease|14|

Lesson 9 - The Way of Prayer

Art by Somkanta Chaterjee

*"Krishna says that whichever mode of worship is followed
if it is done with sincerity, love and devotion,
then the prayer can be considered to be complete"*

Lesson : 9 Adhyaya : 9
The Way of Prayer

When there are so many customs and methods to pray to the Divine, it is sometimes confusing and one begins to wonder what the right way to pray is.

Krishna answered this very question and he said whichever mode of worship is followed if it is done with sincerity, love and devotion, then the prayer can be considered to be complete. Even if we offer with devotion a leaf or a flower or even just plain water, if there is purity and devotion the prayer is acceptable to the Divine.

Sometimes we see that some people pray very peacefully inside a religious place but when they come outside they lose all their peacefulness and sometimes start shouting at others. This is wrong.That is why Krishna said that we must make our actions as offerings in prayer to the Divine.

This way we can be free from anger or sorrow and be always peaceful and cheerful. If we offer our sacrifices as a prayer, we won't feel the burden or any loss in the sacrifice. Even in our happy moments or even while making donations or helping others, if we offer our actions we can experience a sense of freedom. If we can remain this way, we will never have to worry about what 'Good' or 'Evil' is and we can follow our inner call and realize our true potential and destiny.

***

Canto IX: **The Knowledge Supreme-the Secret of Secrets**

अथनवमोऽध्यायः।

atha navamodhyāyaḥ

पत्रं पुष्पं फलं तोयं यो मे भक्त्या प्रयच्छति।
तदहं भक्त्युपहृतमश्नामि प्रयतात्मनः॥९-२६॥

patraṃ puṣpaṃ phalaṃ toyaṃ yo me bhaktyā prayacchati
tad ahaṃ bhaktyupahṛtam aśnāmi prayatātmanaḥ 9.26

He who offers with devotion a leaf or a flower
Or even a singular cup of water
When the offering is with love replete
It is to Me acceptable and complete|26|

यत्करोषि यदश्नासि यज्जुहोषि ददासि यत् ।
यत्तपस्यसि कौन्तेय तत्कुरुष्व मदर्पणम्॥९-२७॥

yat karoṣi yad aśnāsi yaj juhoṣi dadāsi yat
yat tapasyasi kaunteya tat kuruṣva madarpaṇam 9.27

Your sacrifice, your enjoyment and your every action
All your austerities, offerings and your every donation
Channel your soul's effort and its inner will
Let all your offerings be as per my Divine will.|27|

शुभाशुभफलैरेवं मोक्ष्यसे कर्मबन्धनैः ।
संन्यासयोगयुक्तात्मा विमुक्तो मामुपैष्यसि ॥९-२८॥

śubhāśubhaphalair evaṃ mokṣyase karmabandhanaiḥ
saṃnyāsayogayuktātmā vimukto mām upaiṣyasi 9.28

From good and evil, you shall attain liberation
And from the bonds of *Karma*, you shall attain dissolution
With your soul engaged purely in My consecration
You shall be free and experience My realization|28|

***

Lesson 10 - Recognizing the Divine in Nature

Art by Somkanta Chaterjee

" The best qualities in nature are feminine and they are glory, eloquence of speech, sharpness of memory, wisdom and forgiveness"

Lesson : 10 Adhyaya : 10
Recognizing the Divine in Nature

Krishna said that when a person is aware and knows that there is a Divine and all powerful entity in the Universe that existed even before the existence of the earth itself, the person becomes free of confusion and fear and such a person never falls prey to the ploys of the wicked.

Arjuna then requested Krishna to tell him how to recognize the Divine in the world. He asked Krishna how one could see or understand anything in the world to be Divine?

Krishna replied that the Divine resides inside every living creature big or small and is the cause of birth and death for all. From the outside one can recognize the Divinity in the world by understanding the Divine qualities.

He said that the best qualities in nature are feminine and they are glory, eloquence of speech, sharpness of memory, wisdom and forgiveness. The Divine can be observed in the skill of the ruler and the power of the conqueror, in the strategy of the winner and in the silence of secrets. The knowledge of the Divine is what makes an individual wise and well known.

The Divine is present in all the things in the world that are splendid and magnificent and in all the things that are brilliant and beautiful and is the source of energies of all the things in the universe including the sun.

Krishna then finally told Arjuna that there was no need to know all of his existences and forms if he could understand that the Divine is present everywhere at once and that the entire universe is just a fraction of the Divine.

***

Canto X:
The Cosmic Divine, World-Gods and Their Representations

अथ दशमोऽध्यायः।
atha daśamodhyāyaḥ

यो मामजमनादिं च वेत्ति लोकमहेश्वरम्।
असम्मूढः स मर्त्येषु सर्वपापैः प्रमुच्यते ॥१०-३॥

yo mām ajam anādiṃ ca vetti lokamaheśvaram
asaṃmūḍhaḥ sa martyeṣu sarvapāpaiḥ pramucyate 10.3

He who knows that I am beginning-less,
The overlord of all worlds and peoples, I am birth-less,
Free of delusion-the mortal world, he inhabits
And falls not prey to evil's sinful gambits|3|

अहमात्मा गुडाकेश सर्वभूताशयस्थितः।
अहमादिश्च मध्यं च भूतानामन्त एव च ॥१०-२०॥

aham ātmā guḍākeśa sarvabhūtāśayasthitaḥ
aham ādiś ca madhyaḥ ca bhūtānām anta eva ca 10.20

O *Arjuna*, It is My Self that abides
And within all being My divinity resides
For every living being big and small,
It is I who am the beginning, middle and end of all.|20|

मृत्युः सर्वहरश्चाहमुद्भवश्च भविष्यताम्।
कीर्तिः श्रीर्वाक्च नारीणां स्मृतिर्मेधा धृतिः क्षमा ॥ १०-३४॥

mṛtyuḥ sarvaharaś cāham udbhavaś ca bhaviṣyatām
kīrtiḥ śrīr vāk ca nārīṇāṃ smṛtir medhā dhṛtiḥ kṣamā 10.34

I am for the living, the all ensnaring death
And for the beings to come, I am also birth.
Glory, speech, intellect, and memory- the qualities Divine
And forgiveness are all my best virtues feminine |34|

दण्डो दमयतामस्मि नीतिरस्मि जिगीषताम्।
मौनं चैवास्मि गुह्यानां ज्ञानं ज्ञानवतामहम् ॥१०-३८॥

daṇḍo damayatām asmi nītir asmi jigīṣatām
maunaṃ caivāsmi guhyānāṃ jñānaṃ jñānavatām aham 10.38

I am the mastery of the ruler and the power of the tamer
I am the winning strategy of the invincible conqueror
I am the secret of silent things that are unknown
I am the knowledge of the knower who then becomes known|38|

यद्यद्विभूतिमत्सत्त्वं श्रीमदूर्जितमेव वा।
तत्तदेवावगच्छ त्वं मम तेजोंऽशसम्भवम् ॥१०-४१॥

yad yad vibhūtimat sattvaṃ śrīmad ūrjitam eva vā
tat tad evāvagaccha tvaṃ mama tejoṃśasaṃbhavam 10.41

All creatures that are beautiful and splendorous
And all things that are brilliant, powerful and glorious
I am the source from which their energies come to be
Know them to be an infinitesimal fraction of Me |41|

***

Lesson 11 - The Ideal student

" Ideal students are free of desire and hatred and perform their works as instruments of the Divine."

Lesson : 11 Adhyaya : 11
The Ideal Student

After Krishna explained to Arjuna about all the qualities by which we could recognize the Divine in the world, Arjuna's curiosity was still not fulfilled. So he asked Krishna to show him the full-vision of the Divine in the Universe.

The normal eye can only see all objects that are within the human visible range. Even the sun is too brilliant to be seen by the ordinary eye but when sunglasses are worn, it is possible to see. When Krishna told Arjuna that the vision cannot be seen by the ordinary eye, Arjuna requested and pleaded to Krishna to make it possible for him to see. Because Arjuna was pure hearted and a devoted friend, Krishna made a provision for Arjuna to witness the extraordinary vision.

And then finally, Arjuna saw the complete vision of the universal Divine being - the Vishwaroopam. At first Arjuna was too overcome by awe to react as it seemed like a thousand suns had suddenly become one and the brilliance was too spectacular and celestial. But everything was too vast and powerful that the brave warrior Arjuna began to panic with fear. The peacefulness that he had first experienced got replaced with despair as everything in the universe from the heavens to all the living beings were being consumed by a terrible inferno. Arjuna offered a full body prostration to the hair raising and fearsome spectacle. In a thunderous voice, he heard the form speak to Arjuna saying that he was time, the destroyer of all living things and bringer of death for all those who stand by falsehood. Arjuna pleaded to the form to change and assume a milder form that would be soothing to his heart and mind and then to Arjuna's joy, the form changed and became the more pleasing and peaceful form that he was aware of. This peaceful form then told Arjuna to become free and friendly with everybody and perform his duties with sincerity and devotion so that Arjuna too can become one with the Divine.

These final words that Arjuna heard are most relevant to students as well. Ideal students are free of desire and hatred and perform their works as instruments of the Divine.

Canto XI:
The Full Vision of the Universal-Divine Being

अथ एकादशोऽध्यायः।

athaikādaśodhyāyaḥ

दिवि सूर्यसहस्रस्य भवेद्युगपदुत्थिता ।
यदि भाः सदृशी सा स्याद्भासस्तस्य महात्मनः ॥११ -१२॥

divi sūryasahastrasya bhaved yugapad utthitā
yadi bhāḥ sadṛśī sā syād bhāsas tasya mahātmanaḥ 11.12

As if a thousand suns had together emerged
And their brilliance had coalesced and merged
So was the Divine's glorious refulgence,
So overwhelming was the heavenly magnificence|12|

तत्रैकस्थं जगत्कृत्स्नं प्रविभक्तमनेकधा।
अपश्यद्देवदेवस्य शरीरे पाण्डवस्तदा ॥११-१३॥

tatraikastham jagat kṛtsnam pravibhaktam anekadhā
apaśyad devadevasya śarīre pāṇḍavas tadā 11.13

And *Arjuna* was struck with awe
As in the very mortal envelope of *Krishna* he saw
The vision of the God of Gods supreme
The mighty creator of existence's every realm.|13|

नभःस्पृशं दीप्तमनेकवर्णं व्यात्ताननं दीप्तविशालनेत्रम्।
दृष्ट्वा हि त्वां प्रव्यथितान्तरात्मा धृतिं न विन्दामि शमंच विष्णो॥११-२४॥

nabhaḥspṛśaṃ dīptam anekavarṇaṃ vyāttānanaṃ dīptaviśālanetram
dṛṣṭvā hi tvāṃ pravyathitāntarātmā dhṛtiṃ na vindāmi
śamaṃ ca viṣṇo 11.24

Blazing the heavens, is Thy burning manifestation
Multihued, open mouthed with eyes in every dimension
Thy vision I am unable to grasp with joy or peace
For the panic within me does not seem to cease.|24|

श्रीभगवानुवाच।
कालोऽस्मि लोकक्षयकृत्प्रवृद्धो लोकान्समाहर्तुमिह प्रवृत्तः।
ऋतेऽपि त्वां न भविष्यन्ति सर्वे येऽवस्थिताः प्रत्यनीकेषु योधाः ॥११-३२॥

śrībhagavān uvāca
kālosmi lokakṣayakṛt pravṛddho lokān samāhartum iha pravṛttaḥ
ṛtepi tvāṃ na bhaviṣyanti sarve yevasthitāḥ
pratyanīkeṣu yodhāḥ 11.32

Lord *Krishna* spoke:-
"I am time- harbinger of destruction of every thing
I am the colossal destroyer of all that is living
Even without you, these warriors shall not live
To the ranks of the opposing forces, only death I shall give"|32|

मत्कर्मकृन्मत्परमो मद्भक्तः सङ्गवर्जितः।
निर्वैरः सर्वभूतेषु यः स मामेति पाण्डव ॥११-५५॥

matkarmakṛn matparamo madbhaktaḥ saṇgavarjitaḥ
nirvairaḥ sarvabhūteṣu yaḥ sa mām eti pāṇḍava 11.55

O *Arjuna*, Surrender to Me, perform My bidding
Become My devotee and an instrument of My working
With an enmity towards none, from desires become free
Accept Me-My way, for such a man shall only come to Me|55|"

***

Lesson 12 - The Yoga of the Devotee

Art by Priti Pandurangan

"The mode of worship is not so important as compared to the devotion and faith of the worshiper"

Lesson : 12 Adhyaya : 12
The Yoga of the Devotee

Filled with love and a deep sense of gratitude for having witnessed the full vision of the Divine, Arjuna asked Krishna a very important question on devotion. He asked Krishna to tell him who the greatest devotee was. Was it the worshipper of the formed Divine or the worshipper of the formless infinite?

Krishna replied that the mode of worship is not so important as compared to the devotion and faith of the worshipper.He explained to Arjuna that the best of his devotees are those who can keep their minds steady and offer their complete faith without doubts in devotion to the Divine. Krishna then offered Arjuna three options if he found it difficult to always focus on the Divine.

The Three Choices:

1) Krishna told Arjuna that if he could not keep his mind firm and stable in a state of devotion to the Divine, he should practice Yoga and with practice make his mind firm and stable

2) If the practice of Yoga too was difficult, then he should perform all his actions for the sake of the Divine. When all works are done as offerings perfection can be attained in work.

3) If always thinking of the Divine at all times while at work was not possible, then he could at least try to exercise self-control and only renounce the fruits of the actions.

Now these three choices that were presented to Arjuna are also very much available for all of us too. Each can choose as per one's nature. If we want to become Divine in life, we must keep our mind steadily focussed on the Divine in all actions. If we want to attain perfection in all our works, we must perform all our actions as offerings to the Divine. And if we want to be ever joyous and free, we must offer the results of all our actions to the Divine.

Those who choose one of above three options are always peaceful in life and they have no enmity against anybody. They feel a universal love for all and are friends of everybody. They never have ego and ownership issues and they neither disturb others nor do they get disturbed by others.

Krishna then told Arjuna about whom the Divine considers as the dearest Devotee. Krishna said that the dearest one is the one whose sole aim in life is to love the Divine. He said such a person follows the teachings of the Divine and the life of such a person is an example for the entire humanity.

***

Canto XII: **The Yoga of the Devotee:**

अथ द्वादशोऽध्यायः |
atha dvādaśodhyāyaḥ

अर्जुन उवाच ।
एवं सततयुक्ता ये भक्तास्त्वां पर्युपासते ।
ये चाप्यक्षरमव्यक्तं तेषां के योगवित्तमाः ॥१२-१॥

arjuna uvāca
evaṃ satatayuktā ye bhaktās tvāṃ paryupāsate
ye cāpy akṣaram avyaktaṃ teṣāṃ ke yogavittamāḥ 12.1

Arjuna asked:
There exist devotees who constantly seek Thee,
But who has the greatest knowledge of *Yoga*, according to Ye,
Those who worship the form of Thy Divine manifestation,
Or those who seek Thee-the formless unmanifest with devotion?|1|

श्री भगवान उवाच।
मय्यावेश्य मनो ये मां नित्ययुक्ता उपासते ।
श्रद्धया परयोपेतास्ते मे युक्ततमा मताः ॥१२-२॥

śrībhagavān uvāca
mayy āveśya mano ye māṃ nityayuktā upāsate
śraddhayā parayopetāḥ te me yuktatamā matāḥ 12.2

Sri *Krishna* spoke:
"Those who affix their mind's concentration-
And seek verily only My union
With the most supreme faith, who offer Me their prayers
I hold them to be the best amongst My seekers.|2|

अथ चित्तं समाधातुं न शक्नोषि मयि स्थिरम्।
अभ्यासयोगेन ततो मामिच्छाप्तुं धनञ्जय ॥१२-९॥

atha cittaṃ samādhātuṃ na śaknoṣi mayi sthiram
abhyāsayogena tato mām ichāptuṃ dhanaṃjaya 12.9

If to dwell in Me O *Arjuna*, you are not capable
And cannot keep your mind firm and stable
Then by practicing *Yoga* make yourself able
And make your awakened consciousness sustainable|9|

अभ्यासेऽप्यसमर्थोऽसि मत्कर्मपरमो भव।
मदर्थमपि कर्माणि कुर्वन्सिद्धिमवाप्स्यसि ॥१२-१०॥

abhyāsepy asamarthosi matkarmaparamo bhava
madartham api karmāṇi kurvan siddhim avāpsyasi 12.10

And If this *Yoga* too you cannot partake,
Then just perform all your actions for My sake
And let all your works be only Mine
For then you shall attain the perfection Divine.|10|

अथैतदप्यशक्तोऽसि कर्तुं मद्योगमाश्रितः।
सर्वकर्मफलत्यागं ततः कुरु यतात्मवान् ॥१२-११॥

athaitad apy aśaktosi kartuṃ madyogam āśritaḥ
sarvakarmaphalatyāgaṃ tataḥ kuru yatātmavān 12.11

If constantly thinking of Me is beyond You
There is yet another thing that you can still do
Tame your mind through a spirited Self control-
And renounce the fruits of your actions as a whole|11|

ये तु धर्म्यामृतमिदं यथोक्तं पर्युपासते ।
श्रद्दधाना मत्परमा भक्तास्तेऽतीव मे प्रियाः ॥१२-२०॥

ye tu dharmyāmṛtam idaṃ yathoktaṃ paryupāsate
śraddadhānā matparamā bhaktās tetīva me priyāḥ 12.20

But the dearest of My devotees is he
Whose supreme aim in life is to love only Me
For he emulates My teachings with perfect devotion
And his life is the immortal *Dharma*'s exemplification.|20|

Lesson 13 - The Divine Feminine

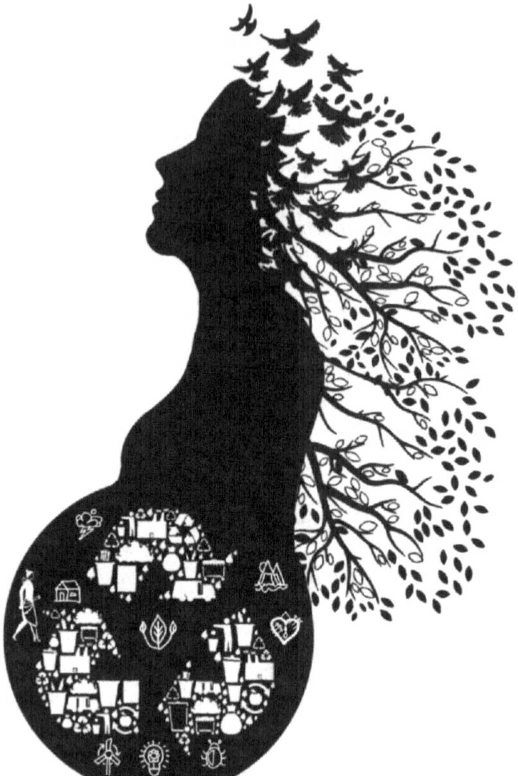

Art by Deeksha Tyagi

"The Creation too is immortal just like the Creator and all living beings are constituents of the Divine Feminine."

Lesson : 13 Adhyaya : 13
The Divine Feminine

Sometimes when we go for a walk in a playground with lots of children playing different ball games at different places, suddenly a ball comes out of nowhere in our direction. If we are alert, we can dodge the ball but if we are unaware, we may get hit. In a similar manner, in life too we must be aware so that we can never get hit by a shock or unexpected occurrence.

Krishna told Arjuna that our body is the field that we must be aware of and we must understand the body. When one can understand its nature of working, then such a person can be considered to be the wise knower.

According to Krishna, This is the Ultimate wisdom that a person can acquire. He said that the Field includes the individual and the five elements (earth, fire, wind, water and sky) and the body communicates with the universe through ten senses and the mind.The ten senses include five senses of wisdom i.e eyes, ears, nose, tongue and skin and the five sense of action ie. speaking/talking, touching/grasping, walking, excreting and reproducing. Krishna told Arjuna that understanding our own body and mind is the foremost that one must do.
The Divine Feminine:

Krishna told Arjuna to understand the duality that exists in the Universe i.e The Creator and the Creation also known in Sanskrit as Purusha and Prakriti. As per the Gita, The Creation is feminine by nature and is called Divine Feminine. It is from her that all the qualities of the nature with its perfections and imperfections originate. The Creation too is immortal just like the Creator and all living beings are constituents of the **Divine Feminine.**

Inside every living individual irrespective of any discrimination, there is the Divine being and thus within the mortal frame the immortal Divine resides.Whoever can see and understand this is the wise knower and such a person can truly see and know the truth. He understands that just like the velocity of the wind in the centre of a storm is zero, behind all the chaos and activity in the play of forces in the universe there is a silent Supreme being. As per the Gita, such a person is not burnt by the flames of passion and for such a person the greatest status is certainly assured.

***

Canto XIII: **The Knower, The Field and Its Divisions**

अथ त्रयोदशोऽध्यायः ।
atha trayodaśodhyāyaḥ

श्रीभगवानुवाच।
इदं शरीरं कौन्तेय क्षेत्रमित्यभिधीयते।
एतद्यो वेत्ति तं प्राहुः क्षेत्रज्ञ इति तद्विदः ॥१३-१॥

śrībhagavān uvāca
idaṃ śarīraṃ kaunteya kṣetram ity abhidhīyate
etad yo vetti taṃ prāhuḥ kṣetrajña iti tadvidaḥ 13.1

Sri Krishna said:
"O Arjuna, this physical body that you own
Is the Field that is to be known
And he who knows in principle its foundation
Is the knower who knows its mode of operation|1|

तत्क्षेत्रं यच्च यादृक्च यद्विकारि यतश्च यत् ।
स च यो यत्प्रभावश्च तत्समासेन मे शृणु ॥१३-३॥

tat kṣetraṃ yac ca yādṛk ca yadvikāri yataś ca yat
sa ca yo yatprabhāvaś ca tat samāsena me śṛṇu 13.3

As the Knower supreme, recognize Me
Knower of all the fields that can in existence be.
The knowledge of the knower and the field
Is the ultimate wisdom that a being can wield.|3|

महाभूतान्यहङ्कारो बुद्धिरव्यक्तमेव च।
इन्द्रियाणि दशैकं च पञ्च चेन्द्रियगोचराः ॥१३-५॥

mahābhūtāny ahaṃkāro buddhir avyaktam eva ca
indriyāṇi daśaikaṃ ca pañca cendriyagocarāḥ 13.5

The field consists of the ego and the five elements,
The mind, the ten senses, their five sense components
Of touch, taste, smell, sound and sight-
And also the inextensible and unmanifest light |5|

प्रकृतिं पुरुषं चैव विद्ध्यनादी उभावपि।
विकारांश्च गुणांश्चैव विद्धि प्रकृतिसम्भवान् ॥१३-१९॥

prakṛtiṃ puruṣaṃ caiva viddhy anādi ubhāv api
vikārāñś ca guṇāṃś caiva viddhi prakṛtisaṃbhavān 13.19

Thus the realm of the field, I have surmised and shown
And also what is knowledge and what is to be known
When My devotees can know this and realize
Then into their natures, My Divinity they materialize.|19|

समं सर्वेषु भूतेषु तिष्ठन्तं परमेश्वरम्।
विनश्यत्स्वविनश्यन्तं यः पश्यति स पश्यति ॥१३-२७॥

samaṃ sarveṣu bhūteṣu tiṣṭhantaṃ paramcśvaram
vinaśyatsv avinaśyantaṃ yaḥ paśyati sa paśyati 13.27

Seated within all life forms is the one Supreme
Residing equally in all beings of the mortal realm
In a perishable frame the indestructible dwells to be
Whoever can thus see, he is the one who can truly see |27|

समं पश्यन्हि सर्वत्र समवस्थितमीश्वरम् ।
न हिनस्त्यात्मनात्मानं ततो याति परां गतिम्॥१३-२८॥

samaṃ paśyan hi sarvatra samavasthitam īśvaram
na hinasty ātmanātmānaṃ tato yāti parāṃ gatim 13.28

***

Lesson 14 - The Three Gunas/ Qualities in Nature

"We must learn to control our Restless Nature and our Lazy Nature and try to increase our Peaceful Nature."

Lesson : 14 Adhyaya : 14
The Three Gunas / Qualities in Nature

Krishna then told Arjuna that the key to understanding Nature was in recognizing the underlying threefold qualities that exist in Nature. He called them as Rajas or the Restless Nature, Tamas or the Lazy Nature and Sattva or the peaceful Nature.

In a person with an increased rajas quality of nature, there is passionate fire for doing things, a restlessness for action,strong opinion about likes and dislikes, a desire for possession and attachment to works.When Rajas nature dominates the passion for doing things becomes converted into desire and greed for acquiring more and more. This greed brings only pain and destruction.

When the tamas quality in a person supersedes, the person gets attached to laziness, casualness, laxity and inertia.Such a person prefers to sleep rather than perform any action and is lost in his own vanity and ignorance.Nothing beneficial ever comes out of this Nature,

Sattva quality is dominant in a person who is virtuous and pure and reflects over and performs actions sincerely. Such a man is least prone to any disease and he is always happy, peaceful and fascinated to gain knowledge.

If we can observe ourselves, we can see that at all three qualities i.e the Restless Nature, the Lazy Nature and the peaceful nature are present inside us and dominate at one point or the other. We must learn to control our Restless Nature and our Lazy Nature and try to increase our Peaceful Nature.

A person with Sattva Nature can ascend and reach the highest state. A person with Rajas Nature remains in the middle but does not descend whereas the person with tamas only descends and sinks into decadence.

Arjuna asked Krishna as to what were the qualities by which one could recognize a person who had transcended all the three natures. Krishna replied that when you see a person who is poised and calm in times of sorrow as well as in times of joy and he treats stone, mud and gold as one and treats praise and blame, friendship and enmity equally, you can understand that such a person has transcended the mortal nature and is truly Divine.

Canto XIV: **The Three Modes of Nature:**

अथ चतुर्दशोऽध्यायः ।

atha caturdaśodhyāyaḥ

सत्त्वं रजस्तम इति गुणाः प्रकृतिसम्भवाः ।
निबध्नन्ति महाबाहो देहे देहिनमव्ययम् ॥१४-५॥

sattvaṃ rajas tama iti guṇāḥ prakṛtisambhavāḥ
nibadhnanti mahābāho dehe dehinam avyayam 14.5

Rajas, *Tamas* and *Sattwa* are the qualities procreated
Three fold in nature they have been created
O *Arjuna,* The immutable Self is bythem bound
Governing the body and consciousness they are found.|5|

तत्र सत्त्वं निर्मलत्वात्प्रकाशकमनामयम् ।
सुखसङ्गेन बध्नाति ज्ञानसङ्गेन चानघ ॥१४-६॥

tatra sattvaṃ nirmalatvāt prakāśakam anāmayam
sukhasaṇgena badhnāti jñānasaṇgena cānagha 14.6

Sattwa is the quality that reflects in serenity,
Illumined by virtue and an immaculate purity.
This quality produces in man no disease or affliction,
O Arjuna! It expresses through happiness
and knowledge's fascination|6|

रजो रागात्मकं विद्धि तृष्णासङ्गसमुद्भवम् ।
तन्निबध्नाति कौन्तेय कर्मसङ्गेन देहिनम् ॥१४-७॥

rajo rāgātmakaṃ viddhi tṛṣṇāsaṇgasamudbhavam
tan nibadhnāti kaunteya karmasaṇgena dehinam 14.7

Rajas is that which ignites in one a passionate fire
A strong feeling of liking, longing and desire
O *Arjuna* it is borne out of a possession for things
Through attachment to works, it binds the *Self* in all beings|7|

तमस्त्वज्ञानजं विद्धि मोहनं सर्वदेहिनाम्।
प्रमादालस्यनिद्राभिस्तन्निबध्नाति भारत ॥१४-८॥

tamas tv ajñānajaṃ viddhi mohanaṃ sarvadehinām
pramādālasyanidrābhis tan nibadhnāti bhārata 14.8

But *Tamas* is the quality that creates a delusion
And traps all beings by ignorance's illusion
O *Arjuna*, the mortals are by it confounded
In laxity, laziness and sleep it is founded|8|

अर्जुनउवाच।
कैर्लिङ्गैस्त्रीन्गुणानेतानतीतो भवति प्रभो ।
किमाचारः कथं चैतांस्त्रीन्गुणानतिवर्तते ॥१४-२१॥

arjuna uvāca
kair liṅgais trīn guṇān etān atīto bhavati prabho
kimācāraḥ kathaṃ caitāṃs trīn guṇān ativartate 14.21

Arjuna asked:
"What are the signs that one can see?
And what are the actions of that soul free?
The triple natures, How does one ascend?
O Lord, Answers to these questions- please extend."|21|

श्रीभगवानुवाच।
प्रकाशं च प्रवृत्तिं च मोहमेव च पाण्डव ।
न द्वेष्टि सम्प्रवृत्तानि न निवृत्तानि काङ्क्षति ॥१४-२२॥

śrībhagavān uvāca
prakāśaṃ ca pravṛttiṃ ca moham eva ca pāṇḍava
na dveṣṭi saṃpravṛttāni na nivṛttāni kāṅkṣati 14.22

Lord *Krishna* replied:
"O *Arjuna*, *Sattwa*'s enlightened mode of action,
Rajas's work impulsions and *Tamas*'s delusion-
He who neither detests nor shirks away
Nor desires these vehicles of nature in any way|22|

समदुःखसुखः स्वस्थः समलोष्टाश्मकाञ्चनः।
तुल्यप्रियाप्रियो धीरस्तुल्यनिन्दात्मसंस्तुतिः ॥ ||१४.२४||

samaduḥkhasukhaḥ svasthaḥ samaloṣṭāśmakāñcanaḥ
tulyapriyāpriyo dhīrastulyanindātmasaṃstutiḥ 24

Who dwells in the Self, poised and still
In both joy and sorrow- he remains tranquil
Stone, mud or gold- all as one he treats
Praise or blame, friend and foes- alike he greets.|24|

मानापमानयोस्तुल्यस्तुल्यो मित्रारिपक्षयोः ।
सर्वारम्भपरित्यागी गुणातीतः स उच्यते ॥१४-२५॥

mānāpamānayos tulyas tulyo mitrāripakṣayoḥ
sarvārambhaparityāgī guṇātītaḥ sa ucyate 14.25

To him honor and insult are just the same
The factions of foes and friends – another zero sum game
In all his work actions, his desire for initiating has ended
Mortal nature, such a being is said to have transcended.|25|

***

Lesson 15 - The Divine Purpose of Creation

Art by Deeksha Tyagi

"The universe has a Divine purpose and it is not a product of chance or fluke. Behind all the chaos of activity that floods the world, there is a Divine orderliness"

Lesson :15 Adhyaya : 15
The Divine Purpose of Creation

Krishna explained to Arjuna in this chapter about the Divine Origin of the Universe. He told him that the universe has a Divine purpose and it is not a product of chance or fluke. Behind all the chaos of activity that floods the world, there is a Divine orderliness. He said that All the living beings originated from the divine and that the soul which is present inside every being is just a fraction of the Divine.

The cosmos is illuminated by the light which shines in the stars and the sun and the moon. The source of the light of the Sun and the stars is the same and we can say that the source is the Divine. The oxygen that causes fire to burn and the life force that flows in all living things also is the same which is the Divine.

In our universe there are two types of forms- those that are perishable and the other which is eternal. All living beings belong to the first type whereas the Divine is above any destruction and is considered to be eternal. Because the Divine is imperishable, the wisest and most rational men of the world and also the ancient texts like the Vedas proclaim that the Divine is the "Supreme Self'.

***

Canto XV : **The Eternal Supernal**

अथ पञ्चदशोऽध्यायः ।
atha pañcadaśodhyāyaḥ

ममैवांशो जीवलोके जीवभूतः सनातनः ।
मनःषष्ठानीन्द्रियाणि प्रकृतिस्थानि कर्षति ॥१५-७॥

mamaivāṃśo jīvaloke jīvabhūtaḥ sanātanaḥ
manaḥṣasṭhānīndriyāṇi prakṛtisthāni karṣati 15.7

All the bodies of the living manifest only from Mine
For their soul is but a quantum of my energies Divine
As a portion of Me in nature begins to dwell
And powers their mind and the five senses as well|7|

यदादित्यगतं तेजो जगद्भासयतेऽखिलम् ।
यच्चन्द्रमसि यच्चाग्नौ तत्तेजो विद्धि मामकम् ॥१५-१२॥

yadādityagataṃ tejo jagadbhāsayatekhilam
yaccandramasi yaccāgnau tattejo viddhi māmakam 15.12

For the entire cosmos it is I who am the light
Illumining the creation, I set the world alight
The sun, the moon and the fire – I verily ignite
Know all that is radiant to be only My might.|12|

अहं वैश्वानरो भूत्वा प्राणिनां देहमाश्रितः ।
प्राणापानसमायुक्तः पचाम्यन्नं चतुर्विधम् ॥१५-१४॥

ahaṃ vaiśvānaro bhūtvā prāṇināṃ dehamāśritaḥ
prāṇāpānasamāyuktaḥ pacāmyannaṃ caturvidham 15.14

Life's fire I have instilled and sustained
By which the physical body of every being is maintained
Controlling the inhalation and exhalation of the life energy
The four types of foods, I verily digest in synergy.|14|

द्वाविमौ पुरुषौ लोके क्षरश्चाक्षर एव च ।
क्षरः सर्वाणि भूतानि कूटस्थोऽक्षर उच्यते ॥१५-१६॥

dvāvimau puruṣau loke kṣaraścākṣara eva ca
kṣaraḥ sarvāṇi bhūtāni kūṭasthokṣara ucyate 15.16

In the universe, there are two forms of manifestation
One indestructible, while the other attains destruction
In all the living things- is found the form destructible
But seated high above them all is the form imperishable|16|

यस्मात्क्षरमतीतोऽहमक्षरादपि चोत्तमः ।
अतोऽस्मि लोके वेदे च प्रथितः पुरुषोत्तमः ॥१५-१८॥

yasmāt kṣaramatītoḥ ahamakṣarādapi cottamaḥ
atosmi loke vede ca prathitaḥ puruṣottamaḥ 15.18

As I am beyond the manifestations perishable,
Transcendent and surpassing even the imperishable
The *Vedas* and the world together proclaim-
'I am the Supreme *Self*' they exclaim.|18|

Lesson 16 - The Twin Traits- Divine & Demoniac

" There are two traits found in people namely the Divine and the Demoniac .All persons belong to one of these two categories depending upon their behavior"

Lesson : 16 Adhyaya : 16
The Twin Traits- Divine and Demoniac

Krishna told Arjuna that there are two traits found in people namely the Divine and the Demoniac. All persons belong to one of these two categories depending upon their behavior.

Whenever people gather in any social gathering, you will see that people with similar minds gather together depending upon their natures. One group consists of people who are talking with sincerity and purity to do good. They dedicate there time for purifying themselves. These people are bereft of anger and are truthful and practise non-violence. They never find faults with others. They are peaceful and devoid of greed. They feel compassion for all. They show modesty, tenderness and an unswerving determination. Such people radiate purity and are always balanced and without envy and pride. These people are said to be having a divine nature.

The other group consists of folks who always boast about themselves and recognize each other by the qualities of egoism, pride and arrogance. This group allows each other's arrogant ego to swell up and enjoy each other's company. They strongly state that there is no truth or God in this world. The world is a creation of mere chance and that everything in this world is moved by desire. They all are always busy grabbing power and money. They consider themselves as enjoyers of desire and they only focus on how to increase wealth and power. They get trapped in the web of lust and desire and forget the meaning of right action. Such people are found to be always worried and they find both good and God to be detestable, Sri Krishna said in the Gita that such unfortunate persons can be said to have a Demoniac Nature.

The Three Gates of Darkness:

Desire, rage and lust are three gates to darkness and destruction. Those with Demoniac nature get trapped in these three gates. But those with the Divine nature renounce desire, rage and lust and hence they can always be free.

***

Canto XVI : **The Divine and the Demoniac**

अथ षोडशोऽध्यायः ।
athaṣoḍaśodhyāyaḥ

श्रीभगवानुवाच।
अभयं सत्त्वसंशुद्धिर्ज्ञानयोगव्यवस्थितिः ।
दानं दमश्च यज्ञश्च स्वाध्यायस्तप आर्जवम् ॥१६-१॥

Śrī bhagavānuvāca
abhayaṃ sattvasaṃśuddhirjñānayogavyavasthitiḥ
dānaṃ damaśca yajñaśca svādhyāyas tapa ārjavam 16.1

Lord Krishna spoke:
Fearlessly persevering for the inner purification
And engaging in the *Yoga* of knowledge with dedication
Holding all the senses in control and by selflessly giving
Engaging in sacrifice, askesis and scriptural reading|1|

अहिंसा सत्यमक्रोधस्त्यागः शान्तिरपैशुनम् ।
दया भूतेष्वलोलुप्त्वं मार्दवं ह्रीरचापलम् ॥१६-२॥

ahiṃsā satyamakrodhastyāgaḥ śāntirapaiśunam
dayā bhūteṣvaloluptvaṃ mārdavaṃ hrīr acāpalam 16.2

Bereft of anger, practicing non-violence and truthfulness
Self giving, absence of faultfinding and peacefulness
Devoid of greed and holding a global compassion
Modesty, tenderness and an unswerving determination.|2|

तेजः क्षमा धृतिः शौचमद्रोहो नातिमानिता ।
भवन्ति सम्पदं दैवीमभिजातस्य भारत ॥१६-३॥

tejaḥ kṣamā dhṛtiḥ śaucamadroho nātimānitā
bhavanti saṃpadaṃ daivīmabhijātasya bhārata 16.3

Radiating purity, showing forgiveness and valiance
Not having envy or pride and holding a poised balance
O *Arjuna*, these qualities encompass the treasure
Inherited by those born with the Divine nature.|3|

दम्भो दर्पोऽभिमानश्च क्रोधः पारुष्यमेवच।
अज्ञानं चाभिजातस्य पार्थ सम्पदमासुरीम् ॥१६-४॥

dambho darpobhimānaśca krodhaḥ pāruṣyameva ca
ajñānaṃ cābhijātasya pārtha saṃpadamāsurīm 16.4

Egoism, false pride and a deceitful arrogance
Anger, harshness and the vice of ignorance
O *Arjuna* these are the qualities that define
Those born with the demoniac nature-undivine.|4|

दैवी सम्पद्विमोक्षाय निबन्धायासुरी मता ।
मा शुचः सम्पदं दैवीमभिजातोऽसि पाण्डव ॥१६-५॥

daivī saṃpadvimokṣāya nibandhāyāsurī matā
mā śucaḥ saṃpadaṃ daivīmabhijātosi pāṇḍava 16.5

By these qualities Divine, liberation one can gain
But demoniac-nature ties one to bondage's chain
O *Arjuna*, Be not under any duress
It is the Divine qualities that you possess.|5|

प्रवृत्तिं च निवृत्तिं च जना न विदुरासुराः।
न शौचं नापि चाचारो न सत्यं तेषु विद्यते ॥१६-७॥

pravṛttiṃ ca nivṛttiṃ ca janā na vidurāsurāḥ
na śaucaṃ nāpi cācāro na satyaṃ teṣu vidyate 16.7

The demoniac beings are ignorant of the right action
Devoid of knowledge and unaware of the path of abstention
There exists no truth in any of these beings
Nor is faithfulness observed in their dealings.|7|

असत्यमप्रतिष्ठं ते जगदाहुरनीश्वरम्।
अपरस्परसम्भूतं किमन्यत्कामहैतुकम् ॥१६-८॥

asatyamapratiṣṭhaṃ te jagadāhuranīśvaram
aparasparasaṃbhūtaṃ kimanyatkāmahaitukam 16.8

"There is No God"- they jubiliantly proclaim
"There is no truth in this world"- so they claim
The origins of the world they dismiss as mere chance
"Only desire is its sole foundation"-Thus is their stance.|8|

कामममाश्रित्य दुष्पूरं दम्भमानमदान्विताः ।
मोहाद्गृहीत्वासद्ग्राहान्प्रवर्तन्तेऽशुचिव्रताः॥ १६-१०॥

kāmamāśritya duṣpūraṃ dambhamānamadānvitāḥ
mohādgṛhītvāsadgrāhānpravartanteśucivratāḥ 16.10

With arrogance and a lust that is never quenched
Their devious minds in egos are drenched
A philosophy of ignorance fuels their desires
And to grab power, their mind incessantly conspires.|10|

***

Lesson 17 - Faith & The Triple Formulae in Nature

"Even the food consumed by a person is of three types according to the taste, liking and preferences of the individual. Depeding on the nature, there are Sattva, Rajas & Tamas type of foods"

Lesson : 17 Adhyaya : 17
Faith & The Triple Formulae in Nature

Arjuna asked Sri Krishna what happens when a person performs actions with the highest devotion without following any scriptures. He asked him what the nature of such a person's faith was. Was it Rajas, Tamas or Sattwa?

Krishna replied that there is a triple combination of natures in every individual. He said that there are shades of all three modes in each individual. Whichever mode is dominant, the individual's nature and behavior is according.

Similarly the actions, sacrifices and even charity performed by the individual is governed by the triple formula. Even the faith is similarly three types. Krishna said that the faith of every individual is distinct and it depends upon the natural instinct of the person. Whatever is the faith of the person, that person also behaves and lives likewise.

Even the food consumed by a person is of three types according to the taste, liking and preferences of the individual. Depending on the nature, there are Sattva, Rajas and Tamas type of foods.

The nature of food consumed by the individual is directly connected with the thoughts as well as the health of the body. As students, we must recognize the type of food that we consume so that we can remain free from ailments and other mental worries.

Sattva foods are those that are succulent, fresh and healthy. They provide nourishment to the body. People of Sattva nature choose this type of food as they want to ensure a long and healthy life. Rajas foods are those that are bitter, salt, hot, sour and dehydrating. People consuming this type of food tend to be very moody and their anxiety affects their health. They often worry a lot and are more prone to ailments.

Tamas foods are the lowermost type of food which consists of stale and rotten food. Only people with Tamas nature eat this type of food and such persons even enjoy eating left over food like animals.

We have observed that of all the three natures, Sattva is the best and we must try to maintain this nature so that all our actions and thoughts become offerings. This attitude ultimately leads to our own betterment.

Canto XVII : **Faith and the Triple Formulae in Nature**

अथ सप्तदशोऽध्यायः।
atha saptadaśodhyāyaḥ

श्रीभगवानुवाच।
त्रिविधा भवति श्रद्धा देहिनां सा स्वभावजा।
सात्त्विकी राजसी चैव तामसी चेति तां शृणु ॥१७-२॥

śrībhagavānuvāca
trividhā bhavati śraddhā dehināṃ sā svabhāvajā
sāttvikī rājasī caiva tāmasī ceti tāṃ śṛṇu 17.2

Sri *Krishna* replied:
"A triple combination of the natures, it may be told
Listen for I shall verily explain their faith-three fold
Whichever of the three qualities is dominant
In that being, that nature of faith is predominant.|2|

सत्त्वानुरूपा सर्वस्य श्रद्धा भवति भारत।
श्रद्धामयोऽयं पुरुषो यो यच्छ्रद्धः स एव सः ॥१७-३॥

sattvānurūpā sarvasya śraddhā bhavati bhārata
śraddhāmayoyaṃ puruṣo yo yacchraddhaḥ sa eva saḥ17.3

O *Arjuna*, The faith in every being is distinct-
Depending purely on the soul's natural instinct
Made up of faith is the inner embodiment living
However his faith is, that way is the being.| 3|

आहारस्त्वपि सर्वस्य त्रिविधो भवति प्रियः।
यज्ञस्तपस्तथा दानं तेषां भेदमिमं शृणु ॥१७-७॥

āhārastvapi sarvasyatrividho bhavati priyaḥ
yajñastapastathā dānaṃ teṣāṃ bhedamimaṃ śṛṇu17.7

Even the foods that are consumed by every creature
Depending on liking are three fold in nature
So too is sacrifice, austerity and charity
Listen to me for I shall explain with clarity.|7|

आयुःसत्त्वबलारोग्यसुखप्रीतिविवर्धनाः ।
रस्याः स्निग्धाः स्थिरा हृद्या आहाराः सात्त्विक प्रियाः ॥१७-८॥

āyuḥ sattvabalārogyasukhaprītivivardhanāḥ
rasyāḥ snigdhāḥ sthirā hṛdyā āhārāḥ sāttvikapriyāḥ17.8

The men of *Sattwa* prefer the following food-
To them all that nourishes and prolongs their life is good.
A succulent, smooth and firm diet they choose to adhere,
For to their mind and bodies, this type of food is most dear.|8|

कट्वम्ललवणात्युष्णतीक्ष्णरूक्षविदाहिनः ।
आहारा राजसस्येष्टा दुःखशोकामयप्रदाः ॥१७-९॥

kaṭvamlalavaṇātyuṣṇatīkṣṇarūkṣavidāhinaḥ
āhārā rājasasyeṣṭā duḥkhaśokāmayapradāḥ 17.9

The men of *Rajas* very much enjoy consuming
All that is bitter, sour, salty, hot, dry and dehydrating
Borne of anxiety and worry they are affected by ailments
And their health is affected by their temperaments.|9|

यातयामं गतरसं पूति पर्युषितंचयत् ।
उच्छिष्टमपि चामेध्यं भोजनं तामसप्रियम् ॥१७-१०॥

yātayāmaṃ gatarasaṃ pūti paryuṣitaṃ ca yat
ucchiṣṭamapi cāmedhyaṃ bhojanaṃ tāmasapriyam17.10

The men of *Tamas* derive a pleasure perverted
In consuming food that is cold, stale and rotted
Foods that are foul, tasteless and even decomposing sour
Like animals, even leftovers they choose to devour.|10|

दातव्यमिति यद्दानं दीयतेऽनुपकारिणे ।
देशे काले च पात्रे च तद्दानं सात्त्विकं स्मृतम् ॥१७-२०॥

dātavyamiti yaddānaṃ dīyatenupakāriṇe
deśe kāle ca pātre ca taddānaṃ sāttvikaṃ smṛtam 17.20

An offering in *Sattwa* is said to be done
Undertaken for the sake of offering, keeping expectations none
Precisely at the right place and moment, the offering is successful
To bring forth the betterment of the recipient, it is bountiful.|20|

Lesson 18 - Equality of all castes & Liberation

"As per the Gita, the caste of an individual is not based upon birth but upon the nature of the individual. All Four castes are equal and no caste is either high or low in comparison to the other"

Lesson : 18 Adhyaya : 18
Equality of all castes and Liberation

The 18th and Final Chapter of the Bhagavad Gita deals with the most important aspect of Moksha or the complete freedom of liberation.

In this chapter, Krishna told Arjuna that liberation can come only by performing one's duties. It cannot be attained by renouncing one's duties. Contrary to popular belief, it is possible to live a liberated and joyous life without having to renounce every activity.

Krishna explained that every individual is free to follow his or her own path that is best suited to the individual's nature. This is because each one can attain perfection through their respective natures itself.

Krishna said that people's way of life is determined by the nature with which the individual is born on earth. He said that there are four classes/castes of individuals based upon the nature of the individual. Thus as per the Gita, the caste of an individual is not based upon birth but upon the nature of the individual. All four castes are equal and no caste is either high or low in comparison to the other.

Krishna described the characteristics that help in identifying the same so that an individual can freely choose his path for attaining expertise. You might be surprised to note that the world's leading career counsellors and psychologists first try to identifying the nature of the child before giving any guidance for choosing a career option.

Those who prefer silence and quietude by nature should be allowed to choose a way of life that suits their nature best. Such persons who like to be calm and peaceful and find great interest in understanding the truth and seek spiritual knowledge can be called Brahmins.

Those who have leadership qualities and derive great interest in fighting and performing heroic deeds must be allowed to flourish in fields that suit this type of nature. Such persons can be called Kshatriyas.

Those who have are talented in the various fields like commerce & trade, fine arts, businesses and agriculture must be allowed to explore and realize their talent in their respective fields. Such persons can be called Vaishyas.

This final class includes one special type of category of persons. This includes those noble hearted individuals who only want to perform service and all their actions get directed for the betterment of mankind. Such types of persons can be called Shudras.

It is very unfortunate that people have not understood this clear and direct message of Krishna. In some parts of the county, discrimination is practiced based upon the caste of the individual and a rigid birth based caste system is followed which classifies one caste as high and the other as low.

As broad minded and global-students, we must not encourage such discrimination and look at all individuals with the same respect as advocated by Krishna because we have understood that everybody is essentially divine from the inside.

We can use these pointers from the Gita to identify our predominant natures and try to choose our paths of life and work sincerely to develop and perfect our skills. This way, we can be truly free and help in making our world a better place.

In the end of the last Chapter, Krishna simply asked Arjuna if he listened to the entire Gita with concentration and asked him if his confusion and grief had gone away. It is very nice to see that ultimately Krishna leaves the freedom of choice in Arjuna's hands to decide his course of action. Arjuna the wise disciple and brave warrior was quick to respond. He replied,

"My delusion is destroyed, my memory has returned
O Krishna, By your grace alone things have thus turned
I am now firm in my resolve, with all doubts cleared
I shall now act, as per Thy words golden that I've heard."

Similarly friends, following Krishna's cue, I would like to ask you "Did you like what you read and heard about the Gita? Will you try to become the champions that the world needs for the better future of man?"

I leave the choice in your hands and pray that all of you be successful in your respective paths of life.

Canto XVIII : **Liberation**

अथ अष्टादशोऽध्यायः।
athāsṭādaśodhyāyah

श्रीभगवानुवाच।
काम्यानां कर्मणां न्यासं संन्यासं कवयो विदुः।
सर्वकर्मफलत्यागं प्राहुस्त्यागं विचक्षणाः ॥१८-२॥

śrībhagavānuvāca
kāmyānāṃ karmaṇāṃ nyāsaṃ saṃnyāsaṃ kavayo viduh
sarvakarmaphalatyāgaṃ prāhustyāgaṃ vicakṣaṇāḥ 18.2

Lord *Krishna* spoke:
"The learned consider *Sannyasa* to be total abstention
From the proscribed duties and actions-an absolute abnegation
But *Tyaga* implies not a complete abstinence
Giving up the fruits of all actions is its key essence.|2|

कार्यमित्येव यत्कर्म नियतं क्रियतेऽर्जुन।
सङ्गं त्यक्त्वा फलं चैव स त्यागः सात्त्विको मतः ॥१८-९॥

kāryamityeva yatkarma niyataṃ kriyaterjuna
saṇgaṃ tyaktvā phalaṃ caiva sa tyāgaḥ sāttviko mataḥ 18.9

He who performs regulated and right actions
Detached and without any fruitive attractions
With a sense of duty, he discharges his deeds everyday
Such a renunciation is in sync with *Sattwa*'s way|9|

नियतं सङ्गरहितमरागद्वेषतः कृतम्।
अफलप्रेप्सुना कर्म यत्तत्सात्त्विकमुच्यते ॥१८-२३॥

niyataṃ saṇgarahitamarāgadveṣataḥ kṛtam
aphalaprepsunā karma yattatsāttvikamucyate 18.23

Any action that is performed in the manner right-
From likings or aversion, by remaining detached,
Regulated and to the fruits of work, by not being attached
Know such actions to be done in *Sattwa*'s light|23|

ब्राह्मणक्षत्रियविशां शूद्राणां च परन्तप।
कर्माणि प्रविभक्तानि स्वभावप्रभवैर्गुणैः ॥१८-४१॥

brāhmaṇakṣatriyaviśāṃ śūdrāṇāṃ ca paraṃtapa
karmāṇi pravibhaktāni svabhāvaprabhavairguṇaiḥ 18.41

Depending wholly on their birth nature
There are the quadruple divisions of equal stature
Based on the individual's tendencies and innate aspects.
Brahmins, *Kshatriyas*, *Vaishyas* and *Shudras* – the four sects|41|

शमो दमस्तपः शौचं क्षान्तिरार्जवमेव च।
ज्ञानं विज्ञानमास्तिक्यं ब्रह्मकर्म स्वभावजम् ॥१८-४२॥

śamo damastapaḥ śaucaṃ kṣāntirārjavameva ca
jñānaṃ vijñānamāstikyaṃ brahmakarma svabhāvajam 18.42

Performing penance, seeking knowledge with a forbearance
Maintaining self-control with a steadfast perseverance
He is termed a *Brahmin* who is pure, calm and peaceful
For it is in his nature to seek the spirit and be truthful|42|

शौर्यं तेजो धृतिर्दाक्ष्यं युद्धे चाप्यपलायनम् ।
दानमीश्वरभावश्च क्षात्रं कर्म स्वभावजम् ॥१८-४३॥

śauryaṃ tejo dhṛtirdākṣyaṃ yuddhe cāpyapalāyanam
dānamīśvarabhāvaśca kṣātraṃ karma svabhāvajam 18.43

Heroism, high spiritedness and strong physical ability
Daring in battle, with determination and gallantry
Benevolence and a skill in leadership
Such is the *Kshatriya*'s nature that commands lordship.|43|

कृषिगौरक्ष्यवाणिज्यं वैश्यकर्म स्वभावजम्।
परिचर्यात्मकं कर्म शूद्रस्यापि स्वभावजम्॥१८-४४॥

kṛṣigaurakṣyavāṇijyaṃ vaiśyakarma svabhāvajam
paricaryātmakaṃ karma śūdrasyāpi svabhāvajam 18.44

The *Vaishyas* are the craftsmen,
the agriculturists, the cattle-raisers
The skilled artisans, the businessmen and the traders
But the *Shudras* have only one aim in mind
To perform service for the betterment of mankind.|44|

कच्चिदेतच्छ्रुतं पार्थ त्वयैकाग्रेण चेतसा ।
कच्चिदज्ञानसम्मोहः प्रनष्टस्ते धनञ्जय ॥१८-७२॥

kaccidetacchrutaṃ pārtha tvayaikāgreṇa cetasā
kaccidajñānasaṃmohaḥ pranaṣṭaste dhanaṃjaya 18.72

O Arjuna, All that I said,did you intently hear,
With a concentrated mind, by lending your ear?
Has the delusion's veil been lifted?
O Arjuna, Has your ignorance been obliterated?|72|"

अर्जुन उवाच।
नष्टो मोहः स्मृतिर्लब्धा त्वत्प्रसादान्मयाच्युत ।
स्थितोऽस्मि गतसन्देहः करिष्ये वचनं तव ॥१८-७३॥

arjuna uvāca
naṣṭo mohaḥ smṛtirlabdhā tvatprasādānmayācyuta
sthitosmi gatasaṃdehaḥ kariṣye vacanaṃ tava 18.73

Arjuna replied:
"My delusion is destroyed, my memory has returned
O Krishna, By your grace alone things have thus turned
I am now firm in my resolve, with all doubts cleared
I shall now act, as per Thy words golden that I've heard."|73|

***

Testimonials of Students of Class 9 Vidya niketan HSS, Puducherry

My gains: Sugitha. S IX

* I understood that we should work without seeing the fruits of the work.
* How to be free from karma's bondage
* Should meditate to get relaxed
* Should have a self limitation
* Should maintain a balanced Gunah.
* Should reach the God within us
* Should aquire all the Good qualities.

From this Gatha class. I have learnt about life. We have to offer our works to god. We have to lead a divine life. By meditation we can reach your soul. Soul never dies. Our souls tell us what to do or not. We have to lead a life like a good person. We have to not acquire bad qualities.

– Rabin Kumar Brahma.

08/12/17 BHGAVAT GEETHA class.

In Bhagavat geetha class we learn all good habits, discipline and Krishna's butter story. And we know all good things you tell in this Bhagavat geetha class. So in 9th STD all of them like this class and know all good habits and good things we learn.

THANK YOU MAM! By: S. Anand

08 12 17.

Bhagavat Geetha Class

In this class, I am learn more about Bhagavat Geetha and How we can Achive in the Life and How to face the problem then How we improve our skill and behaviour. I was Intrest to learn more about the Bhagavat Geetha. Thanks's for this class. I like this class. When I become Adult I promise I learn Bhagavat Geetha

Thank You BHAVANA MAM

- M. Srunath.

10 Tuesday MAY S.Padmaja IX

I have learned a lot and lot about gita because of Bhawana maam and I was very thankful to her after I attending her class. I have changed a lot ~~before~~. and I have gained a lot mainly the prayer should be prayed sincerely and we ~~used~~ should do a work with detachment · concentration etc..., and I am changing my characters.

– Sapna Sharma · IX

* From these classes, I have came to know about the history of Mahabaratha.
* How to pray in a good manner.
* The three good qualities of Krishna, they were,
  i) Concentration
  ii) Devotion and
  iii) Conferation
* Soul never dies.
* Say truth
* Truth never fails.
* One should observe the nature.
* The nature is peaceful, Restless and Lazy
* Detachment is the excellence in yoga.
* If you have self-discipline then everything is possible to us.
* We should follow the Divine trait.
* Thanks for teaching us and after these classes I feel that I am proud to know this and I will manage in my future generation

The song of the DIVINE

One fine day in the middle of the Warfield
caught in fear, deluded in ignorance
a brave warrior questioned its outcome and yield.
His **sincere aspiration** and **surrender** for guidance with **faith**
Made the divine speak with all his affection
GITA, is their insightful conversation.
Listen oh Arjuna! spoke the divine creator
Secrets I reveal to you of my beautiful creation
Fuelled by the discrimination the conflicts arise
Words have failed to reclaim what is right

And so, to establish Dharma this war you have to inevitably fight
Made out of **5 elements** this physical body that you possess
Pride not, as its just a fraction of my energy with which it operates
5 Senses give you pleasure and temptations
Likes and dislikes are **Mind**'s game and perceptions
Good, bad, right, wrong are your **Buddhi'**s Suggestions
But most superior and knower of all is **ME**
Residing as **ATMAN** within.
As you fail to listen to my instructions
You get caught in the mess of your emotions.
Fear not death, it is nothing but a delusion
You too are **Immortal** like ME and MY creation
Uphold the truth and stand for the right with courage
Drop all your desires, lust and rage

With **Concentration, Consecration, and Devotion** fulfil your Dharma
Detached from outcomes and free from expectations should be your **Karma**

What you Sow, so shall you reap
Focus on your actions, on consequences don't you weep
All in the creation, also that you think, speak, Do and eat is governed by

Satva, Rajas and tamas, The 3 Gunas
Transcend these 3-fold nature to become Gunatitah
Then you will experience Equanimity, free from Pleasure and Pain
Liberation is then what you Gain
Gita, thus is the Divine Guidance
Bliss and Joy, you get if lived in accordance.
But you have **Freedom to Choose**
And so, you sometimes win Or Loose
Secrets of all Champions my Dear
Is to always **listen to the Divine** Near
Gita, teaches us to **courageously fight**
Not others, but **for what is right**

Rise over your fear, ignorance, arrogance and delusions
Don't judge, analyse, criticize others
Discriminate not, never jump to conclusions
Accept, Respect and Adapt to all people and situations
Then you become **Global Citizens**
For your own Joy, Peace and Bliss
Practise **Sense Control and self-discipline** with Ease
Actions when done with complete Knowledge, detachment and devotion

Silent mind when achieved with Meditation
You then become **MY** perfect and complete **Reflection.**

- As perceived by Arnav and Garima Sharma
- Gratitude to Krishna's Butter

Parent's Feedback:

There are many who conduct Bhagwad Geeta class, but the way you all conduct the classes is commendable cause you present the Bhagwad Geeta the way it is to all without making any changes into it. That's the greatness about Krishna's butter project.

- Reema Caskar, mother of Vighnesh Caskar (Student of Krishna's butter Gita class)

Thank you ma'am for the amazing sessions on Bhagavad Gita for children. These days children have very few touch points about value systems in the family. They miss out many valuable lessons on life that we had learnt by being with other family members, especially grand parents and other elders. Though the exposure level of children is high with unlimited internet and devices, somehow as parents and society we have failed to provide them the opportunities to assimilate knowledge and draw values from our own rich spiritual and cultural heritage. I sincerely appreciate Midam Trust's efforts to introduce Bhagvad Gita for children. Renee enjoyed the sessions. After the first session she told me that Bhagvad Gita is like value education. It teaches how to lead life. I hope you continue this effort and all children get the opportunity to learn it.

- Mamata Das, mother of Renee (Student of Krishna's butter Gita class)

Midam Charitable Trust's -Krishna's Butter Project

In 2015 Krishna's Butter Project was started by Midam Charitable Trust, Pondicherry under the direction of its founder Sri Madhusudan Damle which led to the development of a Free teaching module and course book published by Midam titled, "Krishna's Butter For Champion Students" authored by senior Pathologist and ex.HOD, Dr.Bhawana Badhe and student of Sri Madhusudan Damle. This was later translated into Hindi and Marathi language by Sri Arvind Chandorkar, a retired banker and student of Damelji and the same was also published by the trust.

Dr.Bhawana Badhe took it to the school class rooms of the students of Class 8 of Vidhyaniketan School, Puducherry and this became a regular feature at their institute. During her free time especially in the weekend, she conducted more classes and connected with various parents and kids who enjoyed the classes. In 2018, one parent, Mrs.Chitra Torvi, a homemaker, was so happy after observing the positive changes in her 2 daughters that she began to learn the methodology of the Krishna's Butter Project and began teaching to interested persons.

In 2020, Once the lockdown started all schools were closed and Mrs.Chitra Torvi came up with the idea of taking it to the digital classrooms. And the module was adopted to suit the Digital platforms and online batches for children 8 and above were launched for children of all countries and backgrounds. **No fee is charged for these sessions** and all children are accommodated on First Come First Serve Basis. Avanti Badhe and Sushrut Badhe, also students of Sri Madhsudan Damle began conducting separate batches for kids and adults respectively after receiving the training to meet the demand for the classes.

So Far, over 3000 children have benefited from Krishna's Butter project and more teachers and students are joining in to form this movement.

Teaching Module: 19 Lessons on the Gita packed with everyday situations and examples, cartoon illustrations, 99 Sanskrit Shlokas, 99 English rhyming translations based on Sri Aurobindo's Integral Yoga principles of education. The rhymes have been adopted from Sushrut Badhe's book – Bhagavad Gita-Rhythm of Krishna which is already listed in the Limca & India Book of Records. Gita concepts like "working without expectation of rewards", "equality of all castes, genders, races" and "Developing a global perspective" are taught in innovative ways and practical homework like "Karma yoga for home", "Controlling desire while shopping", "Not throwing temper tantrums " etc are given to children. Inspired by the workshops results, many parents joined the project and underwent training to teach this module freely so all kids can benefit from them.

Interactive Sessions with Practical homework:
"Karma yoga during home chores", "Controlling desire while shopping", "Not throwing temper tantrums" etc are some of the homework given to children. Homework is designed in such a manner that the dialogue on culture takes place between parents and children in their homes.

World Record:
On 2nd April 2022, Midam was awarded a world record for teaching the Practical Gita principles to over 3000 children in 19 day digital workshops in the post lock down period. A Free teaching module for imparting Cultural, Psychological & Integral Education values from the Bhagavad Gita to children in India & Overseas

Wish to enroll your child for the free 19 day Gita workshop ?

Interested parents, institutions, please feel free to DM us/ Whatssap: +91 9790635964, 9751076593